3D LIFE

Alexandru Ciuciu-Freisinger

3D LIFE
Copyright © 2016 by Alexandru Ciuciu-Freisinger

Paperback / Hardcover ISBN: 978-82-690692-0-4
Ebook ISBN: 978-82-690692-1-1

I dedicate this book to my precious wife.
Christine

Table of Contents

Foreword

If life was a movie, then what would your movie look like? Whatever the answer, the good news is that no matter how good or bad it might look, you still have time to turn it into a success. Throughout this book, I will teach you how to create the most beautiful and successful 3D movie ever seen, where you are the producer, director, and actor. You are the one who decides when the action, drama, passion and humor starts. The success and impact of the film depend only on you because this movie is nothing else but your life. God gifted you the life you have, but its success is determined by your choices.

Success is not defined by chance or accident, but by contrast; it comes in the wake of a clear decision, whereby a person chooses to obtain it. Very often I hear people make up excuses for their lack of success, justifying their failure, in contrast to others who succeeded. Their words are always the same. Those they speak about are always privileged, have opportunities, the right person at the right moment, born into a family with financial capabilities... and the list goes on endlessly.

Such people know why others achieved success, but they don't understand why they fail because excuses are their motto in life. Whether you are a person who finds excuses for everything, or if you choose to pick success, I have good news for you. God has no favorites. He is not in favor of one and against the other. On the contrary, He created all of us with unlimited potential and all we need to do is access it.

The difference between the person who achieves success and the one who finds excuses, is not opportunity, as you might guess. God created opportunities for each of us. The first type of person mentioned has grown and prepared himself to observe opportunities, when they come, and take advantage of them, while the second type of person is still at the stage where he finds excuses. Things that some see as problems, others see as an opportunity for growth. Some see difficulties while others see challenges. For some, fear is a factor that pulls them back, for others, these are reasons to forge ahead. The difference is in the way opportunities are perceived. If we don't see them as possible routes to success, then we'll never access them. On the contrary, we will miss them, one after the other. A well-prepared person knows that it is useless to wonder if opportunities will appear, but is ready to observe them when they occur.

Every person who lives or lived at some point on this Earth is or has been composed of three parts: body, soul, and spirit. These three together make up the person, just like me or you. All the same, each man's life is sectioned in three dimensions:

- **The physical one** represents your body and is related to your health. How well you take care of your body will determine how far your psychological section can go. Everything you will accomplish in life will be as a result of your bodily function.
- **The psychological one** represents your soul (mind, brain) and is related to your material accomplishment. How well you take care of your soul determines every gain in life. How prosperous you will become, how much money you will make, is determined by how well the mind is functioning. The career, status, position, and everything else is related to your mind. Your dreams, goals, aspirations, and desires come from the same place called "soul". The soul has conceived all that exists and has been created by human hands, therefore, what we achieve will depend on the way we use our minds.
- **The spiritual one** represents your spirit and is related to your fulfillment in life. How well you are taking care of your spirit determines how fulfilled, happy and satisfied you are. These three are

not something you are pursuing, rather they come as a result of your connection with the Creator. You are on this earth for a reason and with a purpose and that purpose is determined by the spirit.

When we talk about life, you're definitely one of those people who desire success more than anything, and this is a good thing because each of us has been created with the capacity to achieve success. Success is what any person on this Earth seeks, regardless of his geographical location, race, culture, and age. For some, success may mean one thing, for others, something else. It is certain, however, that all of us want to become successful people.

The majority of people define success in various ways, however, I want to tell you that for me, real success means more than money, position, career prospects or accomplishments. From where I stand, success is the ability to live a "three-dimensional" life. It means being a successful person in terms of the spiritual, psychological, and physical aspects of your being. If a person has achieved success in all three areas mentioned, then, he is definitely a prosperous, happy and a fulfilled person. For a three-dimensional person, limits do not exist on what concerns the accomplishments in life. These people, not only they live their life beautifully but also prepare for their eternal one. When the spirit, soul, and body work together, the results are excellent.

The purpose of this book is to help you connect the spirit that God granted you, with the soul (mind) and body, which through their functionality, help you create a brilliant future. The secret of achieving a three-dimensional life is developing these three areas. God gave you the body, which is your temple; that's why you must take care and develop it if you want it to work on your behalf. You also received a soul, which must be taken care of, if you want to accomplish significant things in life, and last, but not least, you've got a spirit that needs to grow, if you want to develop the unlimited potential which lies inside you. All these three put together to form a successful person. This means you and me. Therefore, throughout this book, I will help you become the best version of yourself.

God created us with an unlimited capacity. The potential that lies within yourself is as unlimited as those whom you consider geniuses. The only difference between you and them is that they have understood how it works, removing everything that limited them, while you're still limited by your own choices. If you truly want to access your potential, you must start by taking control over your body, soul, and spirit. Capability determines the investment that you make in yourself. Starting from now, decide, to invest in yourself for the rest of your life and you will see that your life will change radically. You will go from glory to glory as the Bible teaches.

The problem that intervenes in the lives of the majority of people and which stops them from living their dreams and having the life they imagined for themselves is that those three areas aren't working together because somewhere a rupture was produced. You can be a prosperous person in terms of finance but miserable in terms of happiness or health. Or you can be healthy but bankrupt in terms of finances. Or you can have two of them but not the third, and still, you will not be called successful because a successful person is formed of three parts and lives in three dimensions: body, soul, and spirit. When these three are not connected, you are living in a continuous conflict with yourself. Therefore, my desire is to teach you how to use them together, in order to achieve a successful life.

Introduction

I want to begin this book with a question: "If I were to give you a million dollars and tell you to use it on what you please, what would you do with it?" The question created confusion in the mind of every person that I've asked. Maybe you believe this is not something you are interested in answering because it's a big "If". But I dare you to think right now and try to give a truthful answer. What would you do with the money if you woke up with it in your bank account? The answer you give reveals the reason why you don't have success, or the reason you do.

Asking this question over and over again to people of all ages, from elders to young, I got a lot of answers like: "Well, if I had the money, I would invest in a business." This is the most commonly given answer because it is important to enhance money. Although it seems wise, the truth is that this is not the best answer. Some have told me that they would not accept the money because they're not ready for it, and others itemized what they would buy with it.

Until now, you've likely wondered, what is the correct answer? First, what you need to know is that the sum doesn't matter. When you heard about a million, you immediately thought of the number itself, the thing that counts less. One million dollars is a small amount for a billionaire, but at the same time, it's a big amount for a poor person.

In fact, the most important thing is the investment, the way in which this amount of money is used. While most attempt to explain in detail why they'd invest in a business, or why they'd reject it, I immediately understand why that person doesn't have the money. Do you know, the reason you don't have the money in question? It's simple: because you're not ready for it. If you had the ability to manage that money properly, then you'd have it, but because you lack the required capacity, you don't.

"What would you do with the money, if you had it in your hand?" The correct answer is: "I'd invest in me!" You see, so many think only about themselves and what they might do with the money. Not too many, if you are ready to have it. When a person is ready for a million dollars, he'll make another 100, at least, because he knows how to think and invest like a millionaire. When someone is prepared for a thousand dollars, he'll make several tens of thousands of dollars, and when someone is prepared for a hundred dollars, he'll make several hundred dollars extra. However, what amount of money can be obtained by a person who is ready for a billion dollars? Several billion extra.

For sure, you've probably thought that you would like to be a millionaire and you'd be satisfied with that. It is not impossible to be a millionaire; on the contrary, all you have to do is think like a millionaire, to choose like a millionaire and act like one. Sounds so simple, doesn't it? Well, it is simple, but only if you truly understand how it works.

A person who has the training of a millionaire will make millions out of nothing. The rest will pass indifferently by a thing which nobody would have thought could bring them money. But not those with the thinking of a millionaire. He will make money out of nothing. You can take him anywhere in the world and he will find a way to make money. Take all his possessions, as many times as you want, and you'll see that he will manage again to end up a millionaire. Why? Because his value and training is worth millions.

Steve Jobs is an example of what it means to have the training of a millionaire. Although he was compelled to leave his own company where he fully dedicated himself, body and soul, he started again from scratch. The day after he left Apple, he created another company, called "Next".

The reason I always tell people how important it is to invest in themselves is because I know the following secret: the ability and potential of a person will always rise to the level of its training. God created all of us with an unlimited capacity. There are no privileged or less privileged people when talking about potential. We all hold an unlimited potential. You are probably asking yourself: "Then why are there so many poor, less creative, less intelligent people?" The answer is quite simple: they haven't developed their potential and capability which lies inside of them. These are not determined by the number of degrees you hold but instead, rely on the investment made in oneself. Diplomas, money, career and so on are the results of the investment made in oneself.

If you also have the desire to create meaningful things, then let me tell you that it is possible. In fact, everything you need to obtain lies within you. All you have to do is access and develop the ability that you already possess. When you invest a million dollars in yourself, you will have a million dollar potential, which will help you earn other millions.

Most of us think about how to make quick money, without changing ourselves in some way. If I was able to live an irresponsible life but make money in the process, it would be excellent. Unfortunately, it is impossible to live a life of spiritual, physical and psychological success, without investing in yourself. The truth is that most don't understand that a person's accomplishments raise to the level of their potential. In other words, if your potential is worth thousands, your result won't raise up to millions.

Imagine a scale from 1-10. If you find yourself at level six, your business will get, in the best case, to the sixth level, but there's little chance it will reach level seven. If instead, your potential is processed and you develop it to a level nine, then your business will rise to that level and never over it. It's the same as in any area of life. Maybe you're an athlete and have the goal of reaching a higher level. The only method is to use the best strategies, in order to develop your potential and thus, to increase your level. Maybe you're just an employee or a parent. This rule applies in every domain of our lives.

What you become is more important than what you win, because what you become, directly influences what you win. Everything you have now is nothing but what you've attracted in your life through the person you became until today. "To have more than you currently own, you have to become more than you are."

Now, before I start, let me ask again: What would you do with a million dollars if you'd had it right now? The only safe investment one can make is that of personal development, which will remain eternal, whatever the market, crisis or economic deficits. Any investment has its own risks. When you invest money in a business, there is a risk of market failure, crisis and you'll lose everything, but if you invest in yourself, you will not be affected by any crisis. The next step, after you have invested in yourself is always to invest externally, such as in your dream, in your career, in your future business.

In this book, I will teach you how to invest in yourself and how to develop your potential. You've probably told yourself: "Oh, but I don't have a million dollars to invest in me!"

The good news is that you don't need to have a million dollars. The million dollars was just an example to help you understand how it works. Maybe you're just an employee, who has decided that life is more than going daily to a job that you don't like. Maybe you're a youngster who has decided he wants to create a successful career, or perhaps a parent who has chosen to be more than a parent. You have unlimited potential, waiting to erupt at any moment. Now is the best time to develop that potential and change your life. You don't have to have a million dollars to invest in yourself. All you need is the money you currently have which is more than enough to ensure your development.

Throughout this book, I will teach you how to direct your life towards success and to live a 3D life, meaning an unlimited one. Often, people tell me that they are either too young or too old, too sick or too busy..., all sorts of excuses for not investing in themselves. The secret that I know and you'll discover when you've decided to work on your personal development is this: the right time will never come because it does not exist. The right time is when you choose it to be. You can, at any time, convince yourself you need more money, experience, time, confidence, strategies, relationships, and growth. Trust me when I say that now is the right time to go and develop yourself, and in a year or two, you will understand that indeed, it was the proper time.

Sometimes, I talk to young people who say they don't have time for their personal development because they want to enjoy youth and enjoy it while it lasts. In their minds, it is the belief that they will never have this opportunity again. Such thinking is the result of mediocrity and limitations. These young people don't understand that life is anything you want it to be. Nobody decides when and how you spend it. Choosing parties instead of personal development shows narrow and limited thinking. I ask these young people: "What about the alternative to party now and also later? Why not fill your life with continuous happiness and fulfillment? God did not create us to have a boring and insignificant life but to spread His creativity all around us and enjoy ourselves, side by side with the people around us. "

Many conclude that life is beautiful while you're young, because later on, responsibilities intervene. This is the mediocrity in which most, voluntarily, choose to live. You have the power to transform your happiness and satisfaction into a lifestyle, but only if you choose to break out of the pattern called mediocrity and improve yourself. In order to have a fulfilled life, you must develop the potential within you, which will represent your passion and motivation in its course.

Mostly, we are led by the burning desire to get involved in other's lives, in a meaningful way. We wonder how we can contribute to their lives, how we can help them change and become better. The key to helping others is by helping yourself first. The greatest contribution and the greatest gift that you can give to those around you is your personal growth and development. If I become ten times smarter, stronger, prosperous, what will happen to my employees, my family, my friends? When we become better, wiser, stronger and more prosperous, then those around us will benefit from all of this. If you continue growing and developing your character, health, thinking, earnings, then those around you will want to become like you. For them, you'll become an example worth following.

You also have the desire to become a successful, sincere, attractive, healthy, passionate, determined, happy, prosperous and fulfilled person. You can become a role model for someone.

1

Choices

The real challenge of life consists in living an exceptional life that each of us imagined or will imagine at some point, whether is about success, career, influence, relationships, happiness, money or something else. We all want to experience what is best in life. But, somewhere along the way, we become stuck in our choices. Isn't it true that you have experienced those moments in which you have chosen so wrongly, that the result stopped you from knowing how to manage afterward? These are those moments when you no longer can find the path to the exit, the light at the end of the tunnel. As a result of that experience, you become discouraged, then give up, or even think of renouncing a particular thing, perhaps even your life.

There are so many people who give up on life due to the fact that they no longer see a path to exit from their own choices, in which they've got stuck. This may be due to addictions, to physical or material losses suffered or due to the choices made by others, which affected them indirectly.

Life is the sum of choices made on a daily basis. If there is something that God has given us, above all else on this Earth, it is the gift of choice. The choice is the one that determines the quality of life. It is the secret of an extraordinary life, and the good news is that each of us has this gift at our disposal. I have it, you have it, we all have it and it can change any circumstance in our life, whoever we are.

Choice is a gift and if it is used correctly, can guide our life in the direction we dream of. Although we might not always be able to control the events in our life, we can still choose what to focus on, what that particular event means or how we can use it to move in the direction we are heading.

Is there something in your life that you're not fully satisfied with? Then it's time for a change. You don't like your look? You are not feeling good about your physical state? Change it! Don't like your job? Change it! Don't you like your experiences? Change yourself, by changing the choices you make, and then the experiences will change. If we want a different kind of life, we must make other choices.

You and I have the possibility to change anything in our life, but in order for this to be accomplished, a decision must be taken. A real, sincere, honest decision, through which we eliminate any possibility that distracts us from fully dedicating ourselves to our dreams or aspirations. Based on this, we will act towards what we have proposed.

You must make a real decision if you don't want to keep living in this way. It's time for a change. However, what you need to know is that big choices begin with small choices. Regardless of the nature of the events, good or bad, positive or negative, we have the possibility of choosing, and what we decide will influence the way we will experience things.

Neither the possibilities nor the conditions of life are as important as choices.

You will certainly know or have heard of people who came into the world in an environment in which they had all the favorable conditions. The family in which they were born offered them all the conditions; they were healthy, household relationships were good, however, they failed terribly. At the same time, you know or have heard of so many people who didn't have anything and the odds were against them. However, they succeeded in a manner that nobody could have ever imagined. They became examples of what it means to have nothing and to choose well. If today, you do not choose how you want to live, then you have already made a choice. You choose to let yourself be driven by what life brings your way, instead of deciding what you will do with the things life brings you. Here and now, you need to decide what kind of person you will become.

Even if you do not have material, financial, physical or educational capabilities, still you can choose well, you can head towards the place you dreamed of. All you have to do is to choose wisely. Everyone in this universe is directly influenced by choices. We are and become what we choose.

The choices that affect our life are of two kinds:

Personal choices => represent our own elections, from which we go through experiences which have negative or positive effects on our lives. Your choices are the ones that contribute to the results in your life; these are actually the sum of all the preferences, both good and bad.

The choices of others => in a smaller or higher percentage, every person around us influences our experiences - as a result of the choices that we make on a daily basis. In the same way, my choices, or yours can influence others. Think of a person who chooses to steal certain personal property from you. That choice that you didn't make, affected you. Imagine a loss or anything else that is in no connection with your choices, but which affects you. These are the moments in which the final decision belongs to you, meaning you decide how you will respond to the experiences. Therefore, you choose how you will respond to each event that crosses your path.

Life has its own way of bringing us all sorts of unexpected things, but in each of these, the final decision belongs to us. What you need to know, however, is that the way you relate to them will determine your experiences. Each choice, starting from the first step in life, had an impact in your life, resulting in actions, moments, and experiences. Choices that you perform on a daily basis directly affect your actions, which in turn, determines your experiences. We act on the basis of the choice we make, and as a result of that, it brings a new experience. Where and how we decide to invest our resources, energy and time will determine how and where we will end up. If you want to know how your life will be in five years, look at the way you invest the three things that you have. Every choice you make will be based on resources, time and energy, that it is vital you manage wisely.

Allow me to ask you the following question: Do you enjoy the life you're currently living? Are you satisfied, content with it? Whatever your answer, one thing is certain: the life that you experience today is the outcome of yesterday's choices, meaning the ones from the past. Choices define a person's life. You will always be what you choose to be. All the choices you've made up to this point resulted in your current situation. The life that you have now. Also, out of all the choices, you'll make in the future, the end result will be your life. The life that you will be living.

If you truly want a different life, then you need to choose differently. I've got two lives for you: a good one and a not so good one. The less good news is about the life that you're currently experiencing. Unfortunately, you can no longer return to the past to change your choices, but what you can do is start with a new perspective and a new vision, following a different future and a different life.

Life is determined by five kinds of choices we make:

a) **Very bad choices**: these will always result in a chaotic life, which, eventually, will determine the loss of all hope and faith.
b) **Bad choices**: will always result in an unsatisfied, unhappy, discontent life, which leads to a miserable day to day living
c) **Good choices**: will always result in a mediocre life, which is neither very bad nor very good, but in between. Most of us limit ourselves to simple and less important things, which have to do, mostly, with us and our loved ones.
d) **Very good choices**: will always result in a quite beautiful life. A happy, satisfied and fulfilled life. It's the type of life in which you live with a purpose and significance. It's a life which you don't limit only to yourself, but one in which you try to have a positive impact on other people around you. It's the life that brings you physical and spiritual fulfillment. From these sort of choices, people have

changed the world forever. These are the choices of people who left a mark in the world and made a difference.

e) **Mixed choices.** Most of us are situated in this category. We have values, principles, and beliefs which are beneficial for a certain area of our lives, but that's about it.

We know precisely the principles after which we guide our spiritual life, but less the physical one. We choose extremely consciously, based on solid principles in terms of a financial approach, but we become less relational.

A successful life is formed from great choices, not just in one particular area, but in every area. If you want to choose very well and redirect your life towards success, then you need to form strong beliefs, not only for the spiritual or physical life but for each area that composes it.

Many of us are pleased with one or two good principles, but when it comes to other sides, we have a deficit and then we ask ourselves why things aren't how they should be. The spiritual life, through which you develop daily your relationship with God is the most important one. However, the other sides must not be overlooked, because God doesn't direct us to a successful spiritual life, but on the contrary, He wants for us to excel in every area: spiritual, financial, relational or social.

The purpose of this book is to help you cultivate good and strong beliefs in order to choose wisely.

What kind of life did you have until this point? Is it the mediocre one, which the majority aims for, or is it the one that makes the difference, and for which very few fight? If you want to live a mediocre life, all you need to do is follow the crowd. But if you want something different, then you have to stop right now and think for a moment what you need to do. Do you really want to keep on living in the same way? Do you believe that the manner in which you have lived so far brought you happiness, fulfillment, success? If you're not sure, look at yourself: at the place where you are, at the percentage of fulfillment, satisfaction and happiness, at your job, physical, mental, spiritual, appearance, at the car you drive, at the house you live in, at the people you cherish, at your friends... Do you think this is the way you want to continue living for the rest of your life? If not, then what do you choose?

Try to remember two choices you made that impacted your life in a meaningful way: either negative or positive. Ask yourself how your life would be, if you have chosen differently. Would everything have been different? You don't have to worry about how poorly you have chosen, but what I want you to understand is the power and influence a choice has on your life. A single choice may change the course of your life forever. It may be a simple choice, such as: you went to that school and now you are totally changed; you went out to eat in a certain place and met the person that became your partner; you met someone who invited you to church, and as a result, you handed your life to Jesus and became a new person. A simple decision which affected the rest of your life. What you do, how you're doing it, how you live, what your values in life are, what your faith, is your pleasures, career, influence, money, are the result of your choices.

Our choices lead to actions, and actions determine experiences that prepare our physical destiny and, eventually, the final destiny, after death. Therefore, choices set destinies. So, if you want to change something in your path, you will need to modify your choices. These are the sources of problems, failures, as well as success in life. These are the decisions which transform dreams into reality, and the good news is that each of us has access to them. Even if you're a simple worker in a business, a director, a beggar or a president, young or adult, all of us have the possibility of accessing them. You have access to them; all you need to do is direct your decisions.

Perhaps you're thinking: "I want to choose what is best, but I am so unimportant", or maybe you're thinking that you don't need to get there. Let me just offer you an example of what it means not to have everything you need, but still achieve success: Nick Vujicic is a simple man, with a lot of negatives, intended for a limited life due to his lack of hands and feet. As a child, he struggled with numerous mental, physical, and psychological problems. He had to endure all the criticism and laughter of the children around him, who ridiculed him because of his disabilities. However, at some point, he had to take a decision about his life. He could have easily given up and concentrated on all the unfairness he struggled with. He could have blamed God, his parents, and destiny, or he could raise his head and choose to make a difference in the lives of those around him; to become an inspiration for those who were experiencing the same situation.

What did he choose? He chose to fight, despite all the odds that were against him. Without hands, with just two small legs that can support him, Nick went to primary, secondary, high school and university. At the age of 21, he graduated Griffith University, with a recognized diploma. At the age of 19, he first spoke in public, then he talked over 3000 times in more than 57 countries, on four continents, reaching audiences of up to 110,000, 000 people. For a long time, he has transmitted information to everybody; messages of hope and love of God. Currently, he has two ONG's called "Life without limbs" and "Altitude means attitude". He wrote books and won numerous prizes. In addition, he is married and has two children. Nick Vujicic is the living proof that it doesn't matter where you start, but by contrast, it matters what you choose and where you're determined to get. All of this man's achievements may be summed up in a single word, called choices.

Many people want the opportunity to take this kind of decision, to end up in such places, but they don't think they can, because of the belief that they are not as lucky as others. They are paralyzed by fear because most have no idea about how to make their life and transform their dreams into reality. Thus, they never manage to make radical life changing decisions that will fulfill their dreams.

I wish to tell you that I want to help you choose in such a manner that you will transform your life. It is important to decide right now that you want to change, and that you will be ready to change no matter what it takes to succeed. Success begins with a choice, the choice to change yourself. A real choice means to dedicate yourself to searching for a solution and reject any other possibility. If at this point you choose to change, then at the end of this book, you will be a different person with a different character.

The real challenge is defined by our aspirations because each of us wants something better. All of us want to live a significant life, through which we have an influence, a career, fame, but few of us are careful about our choices that guide our life. What I truly want you to comprehend is that your life will become what you have imagined when you begin to choose wisely.

In conclusion, don't forget one thing: you are what you are today because of yesterday's choices. Tomorrow you will be what you'll be due to the choices of today. What stands between you and the place you want to reach, the studies you want to make, the career path you wish to follow, the art you want to create, the invention you want to invent, the business you want to develop, the dream you want to fulfill... is you. Choices are those which made you evolve or give up, no matter what you proposed to accomplish in life. You cannot expect to reach the peak of the mountain without proper equipment. You must start equipping yourself with the right equipment for the mountain, and sooner or later you'll succeed. But, as long as your dream to climb the mountain is just an aspiration and not a choice that allows you to act, it will be impossible.

To get somewhere, you must want it. It doesn't just simply happen. If, however, you want to go through life just accidentally, without realizing something, then let yourself be carried away, by what is called survival. To leave a mark anywhere you go, you must make a plan towards this. All this begins with a proposal: to be different, to accomplish something different, live differently.

Before we move forward, I want to encourage you to take a decision now, to change something starting from today. Maybe you don't have a vision or a dream for this life yet, but you need to seriously think about what you truly want to accomplish and what God wants you to become and do. What is your calling and God's purpose for your life? Think about this question and write the vision that you seek and on this basis, act from now on. If you already have a vision, then strengthen it, making sure it's your life's purpose. Maybe it is hard to form a vision for your whole life. Then I suggest you limit yourself to 10 or 5 years.

Where do you want to be five years from now? Visualize this and make a plan that enables you to get there. If this is too much for you, then choose a one year vision. What do you want to accomplish this year? Write it down and remember it daily.

_____

_____

_____

_____

_____

_____

What affects our choices?

We all want a different life, but only a few succeed. Why? Why do most people fail, although they know what they should do in order to change? They all have the gift of choice given by God however, 98% continue to choose in the same stupid and hurtful manner.

I want to change but nevertheless, I continue to fail, despite the efforts invested in change. Why am I not successful? The answer is: because of the factors that influence my daily decisions. Choices are influenced by nine things:

1) Beliefs	6) Thoughts
2) Curiosities	7) Character
3) Emotions	8) Values
4) Habits	9) Principles
5) Addictions	

Although it is likely you've never thought of them, your brain has created an internal system, through which it coordinates and determines your choices. This system acts in the subconscious, directing all our thoughts, beliefs, habits, choices, actions, and senses, both good and bad, in every moment of our lives; it controls each decision and the meaning we give to each thing we experience in life and determines what we do, why we do it, what we should do and what we don't do.

The scary part is that most of us don't realize in our conscious mind, how these things lead our lives and as a result, we never think about a change. Changing for the better each of these nine things, either when we're speaking about beliefs, curiosities, emotional state, habits, addictions, thoughts, character, values, and principles, will get an immediate and measurable result in our lives, reaching different kinds of choices, and subsequently, experiences.

In the next chapter, I will teach you how to manage each of the five things and how to make any kind of change in your character. I will help you understand why you do what you shouldn't and how to do what you're supposed to do.

2

Beliefs

We all have beliefs which are deeply printed inside us, about life, people, ourselves, God, death, society... and the list goes on starting from the most significant things, up to the most insignificant ones. A belief is a collection of thoughts, through which we decide the truth about a certain area, a certain thing, or about a person in our lives. Beliefs are what give us the feeling of safety and comfort. They are imprinted through rehearsal, in the neuronal paths of the brain. Information coming from senses passes these routes in order to be intercepted by the brain. This means that, before receiving an interpretation from the brain, the information received is filtered through our beliefs. In this way, the reality that we perceive is not exact but is manipulated by beliefs. In fact, we decide how we relate to the information received, based on our beliefs.

Beliefs are the alleged truths. A belief never changes if it is not brought into doubt, and for change to occur, there is a need for curiosity to study it and understand if it is real and well-founded.

At the same time, courage and willingness are required in order to walk on a minefield land. This is because, there is the possibility we will be challenged with regard to what we believed for a lifetime, demonstrating either that this belief is unfounded, or that our brain loves the comfort zone in which it is located. Moreover, the brain knows that many of the beliefs which restrict us, in fact, relieve us of the need to take action and seek opportunities, or the need to leave our comfort zone in order to assume greater responsibilities. Other restrictive excuses give us convenient reasons to work less.

It is important to understand that what we perceive as reality, is not necessarily the truth, but it's just a personal version of it. Beliefs will provide a retouched picture of things around us. Whether it is good or bad, beliefs act as filters, disguising any proof that doesn't support them. We filter reality through our senses, language, congenital tendencies, relating them to personal experiences.

Beliefs that form self-image arise from generalizations, many of them unfounded, that you have formed over your life. The reason our subconscious stubbornly maintains them is that it has the tendency to continue doing what it is used to and remain consistent with what has been said and done in the past. Any attempt to change the patterns of thinking and doing from the present triggers a homeostatic impulse, which makes you feel uncomfortable and awkward.

The human brain seeks comfort and pleasure and tries to detach itself from discomfort and pain, and for this reason, when it finds itself in uncomfortable situations, the natural tendency of man is to return to old patterns. This trend is one of the challenges faced by each individual and it needs to be defeated; release yourself from this habit if you want to become productive, active and to free the potential which lies inside you. Get used to the idea of feeling uncomfortable and awkward, if you wish to obtain a higher level of efficiency.

How does a belief take form?

The principle of belief states that what you believe for a long period of time about yourself, others or any other thing around you, becomes the truth for you. You will end up believing everything that you've told yourself, or what was told to you repeatedly. A proverb says that "a lie told enough times becomes the truth".

You don't believe what you see, as much as what you have already decided to believe. For the most part, your beliefs will produce experiences in life, and not vice versa. In childhood, you form beliefs through dominant influences which you were exposed to. For instance, you assimilated beliefs from your parents, professors, friends, or mass-media, but along with them, are the interpretations that you associated with these beliefs which are also inherited.

As you get further along in life, but especially in childhood, you acquire a series of beliefs that are either partially or totally false. Such beliefs limit us and are in a direct contradiction with what the Bible preaches about our possibilities. Once you've set a belief, you tend to observe only those things that grow your faith in that belief. Try approaching a selective perception and you'll give yourself a chance to experience your own version of reality.

Belief is achieved through a wide process. In order for a thing to become a belief for you, it needs to be repeated enough times. The process by which a belief is achieved takes place in the neural systems but is based on the information on a particular thing received by the brain.

Information reaching the brain comes through the five senses, which every man has: hearing, sight, smell, touch, and taste. The senses constantly send information based on what they perceive as an image that can be of two kinds: positive or negative.

For example, if I show you a particular thing, the visual sense immediately sends information to the brain, depending on what you saw. If you smelled a certain flavor or a particular fragrance, the sense of smell will send this information to the brain. If you felt a touch, or if you've hurt yourself again, your sense of touch informs the brain about what it perceived.

The same happens in each moment, regardless of what sense or senses go into action. If for example, I bring a fragrance and put a little on you, immediately, various senses perceive this information: smell, sight, touch, and hearing; only taste does not apply in this situation. Things differ depending on the situation encountered. For any thing, person, event, etc. you have an image that reflects your belief. It is crucial to feed your brain with positive images about positive things. But, if those particular things are not beneficial, you need a negative image in order to reject them.

Once sent to the brain, the information passes through the filters of belief, which intercepts them and sends them forth as a positive or negative images. Then the brain, relying on what it has received, will again send signals, activating the body's senses. In other words, every action that you realize is due to the choices that your beliefs have influenced. You'll always make decisions or choices based on beliefs.

How did we form our beliefs until now?
Until the present time, each of us has accumulated a multitude of beliefs, some good, others bad, and those either set us back in our path and limited us or helped us grow and reach maturity. Where do we have these beliefs?

Imagine that in the five minutes after your birth, someone decided your name, nationality, religion, and since then, you spent every minute of your life protecting something you haven't even chosen. From the moment you are born, the family is the first environment where you form a large number of your beliefs. Later on, you develop them at school, among friends, at Church, and in society.

Each of us has decided daily, up to the present moment, something that others learned and taught us, not something we chose. Most beliefs that will determine your choices don't even belong to you, but to your parents, friends, or society.

It is impossible to choose differently, as long as the beliefs remain the same. Ask yourself if you are pleased with your present experiences. If not, it's time for a change. If you have wondered why your life is mediocre and doesn't seem to have a meaning, then I'll tell you why: because your beliefs are not so good. Therefore, you will need to change these beliefs, to replace them with better ones, based on reality and truth. Your life will never make sense as long as you live it depending on what someone else believes because God created you to be yourself and them to be them. In other words, their lifestyle does not always fit yours, because you are a different person. However, the good news is that you can change this. Do you want to experience that success, that sense of winning, and to fulfill your dream? Then it's time to change your beliefs, because, until this moment, they have stopped you, from becoming the person you proposed to be. If your beliefs are going to change, then your choices will change too, then your actions and finally, your experiences. God gave you a gift that no one can take away: the gift of choice; but what you stack into your brain will influence the way you use it. Make sure that you have the best beliefs for achieving a very good life.

Verifying beliefs

Now that we know how beliefs can affect our life, we want to check each belief, in order to see if it's based on reality, on morality, on God's values, and if they are beneficial. We must establish how it affects our current beliefs. Do these limit our lives?

If they do limit us, it means that we must to get rid of them and create other beliefs in their place. If you're not happy and fulfilled, it means that you have to change your beliefs, because they give you the life God has offered. Beliefs will either lead towards a beautiful life, or towards an unfulfilled one. You and I decide what beliefs lead our life choices. In order to verify and make sure that we build the best beliefs, we have to take them one at a time, each and every one of them and pass them through the specially created filter to ensure their verification. We must proceed in the same manner with every belief that we'll have in the future.

To discover the nature of a belief, we must ask ourselves a few questions, in order to see if what we believe is real and founded on verifiable arguments, or if it's just fiction and manipulation by someone who tries to lead our lives.

The questions are designed for meditating on the confusion that we have with respect to a certain belief. We must do the same with the habits that we've developed so far, or that we want to develop because part of our life is coordinated by the habits that we've cultivated. Each of us has rituals or traditions that we practice on a daily basis, such as attending a workplace, prayer, reading, eating, washing, perhaps cooking, sleeping... These are good habits, which bring benefits to our lives, but there are others which are less beneficial, such as being late, smoking, consuming of alcoholic beverages, gossiping, lying, etc. These are negative habits, which seriously harm our quality of life. If you practice them, you'll need to get rid of them immediately, in order to wisely redirect your life.

Of course, I have illustrated two simple lists, but what I want to ask you is to explore your life carefully, because your habits denote who you are as a person and even reveal your character. Success in life does not happen by accident, but on the contrary, it's the sum of good habits.

To truly discover the beliefs and habits that limit you, that pull you down or even bring harm into your life, then you'll have to make a list following the effects they have on your life. In order to achieve this, you need to ask extra questions, through which their nature will be revealed. For starters, write on a sheet of paper, in a notebook or on whatever you want, each habit that you practice daily.

Personal beliefs are an important and necessary list of the beliefs you have about everything. Beliefs about yourself, about the people around you, society, God, about time management, dreams, achievements you want to fulfill. These are just a few examples, but beliefs function in each area of your life, starting from what you eat or drink, up to what you believe about life. You have to check where you are today and towards what you're heading, what is the goal you chase and what are your aspirations. If you are unhappy with the present results, then you have to fight for a better and qualitative life, replacing the current beliefs.

After you have completed the second list of beliefs you want to change, it's time to verify and pass them through the filter. In the end, you'll have a list of those that need to be changed. In the next part of this book, we will begin to change them.

Filter: consists of three questions that will help you discover the nature of a practice or a belief. For this, we use three models:

a) Identification - What information do I have about the belief in which I believe? This is the first question that you need to address with respect to the information and arguments you have regarding what you think. In the process of discovering belief, you have to look at your daily choices. Through the choices you make, you can discover your beliefs, because, to a large extent, our choices are dictated by our beliefs.

When verifying that belief which you want to test, ask yourself: "Are there plausible arguments for my faith, or is it just a lie, a created illusion?" To discover this, you have to look for the available information about that belief. In the search for arguments, you'll always find two camps that will try to argue about what they think about your belief. You will need to consider both options.

While looking for information, take a sheet of paper and split it into two columns: on one side write "pro-belief", on the other "against belief". In the "pro" column, write down all the positive arguments that you find, and in the "against" section, all the negative ones. Once you stop your search, you'll have two lists. Draw a line under the arguments and compare them in order to see what makes sense and what doesn't. Once the process is done, you will have a conclusion about the most plausible definition and thus, you will be able to draw a conclusion based on the found arguments.

Attention! Checking the belief requires you to challenge something that you already believe and for which you have pro arguments, therefore, in your research do not let what you think influence you because this will manipulate the outcome. You must be neutral until the final evidence is presented, because otherwise, you will influence the conclusion.

You must be honest in their verification and comparison, as well as in the search for arguments. If for example, in looking for the pros, you will seek to be the most prepared person on the market, then the same must be done when looking for the cons, otherwise, the conclusion will be obvious. The person who has the best training will know how to better make a point, even if what he says is not true, and therefore, can influence you to have a belief which may not help you. Therefore, be transparent, don't let yourself be influenced and understand that it is your life that will be affected directly.

b) *Origin/Source* - Does that belief come into contradiction with God's character and morality? It is very important that what you think, does not violate God's principles and morality. If that belief is in contradiction with the morality and values of God, then it should be changed. In order to understand which things are moral and immoral, I advise you to study this area separately. Anything that violates God's morality comes from the devil, that's why it should be rejected, otherwise it will affect your choices and ultimately, your life.

Attention! Christians are different, depending on the environment in which they grew up in. Those who responded to the changes in society, adapt their approaching methods but keep the message and moral character unaltered. I encourage you to choose them as a landmark for checking your moral conduct with respect to beliefs. Some will say that it is wrong to wear a certain type of clothing, or to dance, to have a particular job and or take part in certain activities. No matter what they say, you must check and personally convince yourself. The Bible defines the sins as immoral, for this reason; you need to identify them in your life.

c) *Effect* - after you have verified the information, the next step comes, namely, the practical verification of information. What does the life of people who have that belief look like? Is it positive or negative? What kind of experience do they have as a result of their respective beliefs? Are they moral people, do they have well-defined values, does their lifestyle violate God's morality? How do these people report to those around them, as a result of that belief? Do they care about the people around them, or are they living only for themselves? Are they better? Is their life happy and fulfilled due to that belief? Look at the result of their belief and at the effect it has on their lives. Is it positive or negative? Because you don't want to believe in something that makes you unhappy, unfulfilled and will lead you nowhere!

Attention! These questions will reveal if the information is plausible and practical or just sounds great in theory. For example, there are many people who believe in one thing and sustain it with all their passion. But when you look at the end result of that belief in their lives, you feel pity and compassion for them, because it's clear that it's pulling them down, making them unhappy, unfulfilled. You have to look at the effect of the belief that you're checking, in people's lives.

Example: Let's suppose a person states that smoking is beneficial and even challenges you to try it for yourself, explaining that it reduces stress and calms you down. What will you choose? Well, after you've checked the information in the first part of this book, you passed to the second one, you've seen that it doesn't contradict morality and you get to the third point, verifying the outcome in the lives of the persons who practice it. By doing this, you will get a visibly negative answer, because tobacco produces exactly the opposite result i.e., addiction, stress, it destroys health, causes cancer... and the list goes on. It was so simple to observe that this habit is destructive. As such, I won't accept such a habit.

Another example: Let's suppose you are a person who believes in God with all your being, but you don't know exactly what to think about a certain thing that was communicated. For this reason, you don't know what to choose, or maybe you already have a belief, but you want to see if it's plausible. In order to achieve this, again, you will need to use the filter in question, until you obtain the impact that it has in the lives of the people who practice it.

For a long time, I believed that God wanted me to be poor because this is what I was thought. Because I had a different belief, I lived a limited life, for a great period of time. As long as you believe that God wants you to be poor, of course, you'll not search for a way to grow and you will remain this way, both you and the people you influence. However, at some point, this belief proved to be false, so I changed it immediately, and since then, my life changed. Not only have I become a better person, with good aspirations, but the people around me have experienced a growth, as a result of my influence in their lives. Thus, I was able to prosper, and this prosperity proved to be beneficial to those around me.

You and I cannot be a blessing to others until we are blessed first. In order to help others prosper, we must prosper first. Taking a glimpse into the lives of those who were pro and those who were against my belief, I could easily see the beneficial contribution of the people who believed that God wants us to be prosperous, this being exactly the opposite of what I thought. Surprised, I searched for the second group of people, namely those who believed that God is against prosperity. I noticed that the results of their lives were extremely weak and limited. So, I changed my belief immediately, and since then my life has changed. Verify each belief that you have because it will limit your life. A fulfilled life is the result of good beliefs.

3

Curiosities

There are times in life when we choose without being influenced by beliefs but influenced by curiosity. For sure, you've made a choice life at least once under the influence of curiosity.

As human beings, we need to experiment with new things because they are the things that make a difference in a person's life. Curiosity is the mother of all things, inventions, and all the discoveries that we have so far. Your life is due in part to curiosities.

Curiosity can mean a good and positive thing, or a bad and negative one, depending on how it is used. If used correctly, it leads us towards knowledge, fulfillment, discovery, invention. If used incorrectly, it can destroy your life, leading us towards addictions such as cigars, drugs, theft, violence, abuse, sin.

Curiosity means the temptation or invitation to try a new thing, never encountered before until that time. However, because your brain doesn't have a belief formed about that specific thing, you'll remain neutral, leaving the choice in your hands. Now, if you understand how it can influence your decisions, you need to be more careful in the way you relate to curiosity. Curiosity is part of our life and it's very important and beneficial if used correctly. Always, when you choose out of curiosity, ask yourself a few questions that will simplify the process of decision making and will reduce the risk of mistakes. Ask yourself: if I do a certain thing, or if I go to that location, regardless of the curiosity I feel, then:

1) What benefits will I have? Will it help me? Will I feel good? Is it going to fulfill me? Will it make me better or worse? Will it lead me to growth or decay? What will I win if I accept the challenge? Will it lead me closer to God, or it will straighten my path?

2) What are the risks? Will my values be affected? What about my health? Will my morality be affected? What about my beliefs? Through these questions we address to ourselves, the brain is directed to seek out details regarding our curiosity, making it easier and less risky. For example, if the proposal that someone makes to you (a drug, a certain type of food, a night out somewhere, a certain activity etc.) have not been experienced and represent something new for you, then curiosity can affect your choice. You don't know any detail about what was proposed, therefore, the brain has no belief to base a decision on. Therefore, only one possibility remains, namely choosing out of curiosity. How will you relate to it? Will you try it to see how it is, thinking you have nothing to lose, or will you examine it through a set of questions that will help in choosing wisely? It is absolutely normal to try, but what if you try it and it negatively affects you?

Answering to a set of questions decreases the chances of choosing wrongly. For this reason, don't make decisions if you're not sure, but ask questions to the person who made the proposal to find out details. In doing so, you form an image about possible dangers, but also about the benefits.

At the same time, you can discover the advantages or disadvantages, depending on the proposal made. What is certain is that once the questions are asked, the risk of wrong choices decreases exponentially. Curiosity works for the best, more positively and more beneficially when it is accompanied by wise questions.

What you need to know is that all of us ask questions when we are put in a situation of this type. If, however, the questions are not consciously directed to the topic, then they will be directed by the subconscious, which will make the choice rushed. It is one thing to let yourself be guided by the subconscious, putting nonspecific (unclear) questions, and another to be specifically guided by the conscious mind (the most powerful part), asking questions related to the topic. Choosing consciously means having a principle, a belief, about how you relate to curiosity. There's a big difference between making decisions based on principles, and making decisions on the basis of senses, or what life brings out for you.

"Choose consciously and you'll live eloquently".

4

Emotions

Controlling the emotions of the moment is a discipline that each of us should adopt as a lifestyle. Many people first act and then think. Such a strategy often brings disappointment, because the present state influences a person's choices. For great results, obtained from good choices, we need to learn to think before acting. The first and most important thing you need to realize is that you are in control of your emotions. Nobody can influence your emotions without your permission. People around you, things, circumstances, the place you are can lead to a certain state of mind, but only if you allow this. You are the one who decides what you will feel.

In life, choices are influenced by positive or negative emotional states through which we pass in a certain moment.

The positive state of mind – there are times where you're extremely happy and cheerful, as a result of a positive experience. You're so excited and passionate, that nothing can stop you from doing what you intend to do, or what you dream of. No one and nothing can affect you, no matter what they say. That state gives a positive perspective about the information coming from the brain, blocking the influence of negativity.

The negative state of mind – there are times where you're so down and depressed that nothing pleases you. All around you irritates you, creating discomfort. These are those moments in which the emotional state is so negative, that everything becomes negative around you. Isn't it true you have experienced situations in which you were so nervous, shaken and wounded, that you weren't able to control your emotions and said all sorts of bad words to someone who had nothing to do with the situation you were in, but, on the contrary, tried to help you? After a long or short while, depending on the gravity of the situation, everything returned to normal. You overcame that state of mind, and now understand what mistakes you've made and feel sorry for your nasty and rude actions which created discomfort to other sincere individuals who were only trying to help you. This process is called "present state of mind" and has influenced you without you realizing.

The emotional state can affect us positively or negatively in our decision-making. In order to take the best decisions, make sure you never choose when under pressure. If it happens, and you're in an inadequate state of mind, postpone any sort of decision, because, under pressure, the brain is unable to choose logically. The decision will be influenced by your state of mind and being under pressure, we usually make the biggest mistakes that we later regret and which affect us negatively. Under pressure, you tend to speak rudely to your partner, yell at your children, make costly decisions, losing control of your thoughts. Pressure creates stress and anxiety, and for this reason, decisions made under pressure bring negative experiences along with them. I have decided to never take decisions, as long as I am in an inappropriate state of mind.

When you find yourself in a conversation that cannot be controlled, it is always better to withdraw and return after its intensity decreases, and you have regained calmness. You can be in a conversation with your partner who you love deeply and yet, if you do not change the subject, you will continue in a direction that will affect the relationship. If you can control it, very well, but if you can't, stop it right there, withdraw and come back in a few seconds or minutes; in most cases, there will be no need to continue, because you'll both understand that it makes no sense.

About 90% of relationships (marriage, friendship, family, social, etc.) are destroyed because of haywire conversations. Most conflicts arise from the tone of voice and attitude, and only a tiny fraction of them are caused by differences in opinion. If you subprime your emotions and control your emotional state, then you'll control 90% of the conflicts with your partner. Imagine the pulse you're bringing to the relationship through the harmony and peace that you will experience. Every argument, regardless of its size, distracts from the love's intensity, therefore, your goal should be a positive emotional state in any situation.

If you can't control the emotional state in which you find yourself, no problem, withdraw and come back any time you want. The results will be different. You must understand that your partner, your friend, or any other person may be in an unavailable state, due to things that they are experiencing at that moment; things you may know nothing about. In other words, they are behaving that way due to difficult situations. So, don't be a fire intensifier, but someone who puts out the fire, because, by doing so, you diminish the possibility of burns.

Always remember that people have reasons for being in that emotional state, reasons that you are not aware of. All you have to do is to be next to that person in a positive way, regardless of the circumstances.

Unfortunately, I grew up in an environment in which, when someone experienced a challenge or a problem, most knew why. Some said that he deserved it, others accused him of wrong decisions others said it was because of sin, while others invented all sorts of reasons. Only one or two acknowledged that they didn't know why those things happened, but they were willing to help.

What kind of person are you? People have chosen poorly and continue to choose poorly, but we have an advantage that nobody can take away, namely, to decide how to respond to their choices. Maybe you're affected by the decisions of those around you, and yet, you have the power to change the experiences and emotions through the way you relate to events. John Maxwell said that each person carries with him two canisters. One filled up with gasoline and another with water. In every situation where a fire ignites, you need to choose which canister you use. Use water to extinguish the fire, or gasoline to feed the flames from which you will have burns for the rest of your life?

If you happen to find yourself under pressure, being forced to make a choice on the spot, meaning it's an emergency, and you don't know exactly what to do, then you'd better excuse yourself for a few moments and get out of the room if possible. Sit alone for a few moments, depending on the situation, and meditate in silence. If this is not possible, then head towards a window, open it up and inhale and exhale for a few moments.

When the air powerfully enters your lungs, the brain is oxygenated and takes control of your emotions, giving you the opportunity to use your logic again. If instead, you find yourself under pressure and can't withdraw from the conflict in which you find yourself, then it is vital to stop any kind of contact with the person in question immediately and redirect your focus onto something positive. It can be a beautiful experience from your life, a joke someone told you, or another trivial thing.

There are moments in which the situation you find yourself in is continuous. It could be about a material, financial or physical loss, by which I mean you've lost a loved one, you gone through a divorce, you received an unfavorable medical report. No matter where the loss comes from, it produces much suffering and pressure, things which will influence your decisions. Therefore, to make sure you don't choose wrongly, especially if you have to take significant decisions, find a close person that you trust. A person who is and was beside you and who wishes only the best for you. Consult with that person. All successful people that you see have behind them a mentor who helps them in their decisions. I encourage you to find such a mentor, especially when you find yourself in an unstable emotional state. That person will help you make the best choices and get over any loss or suffering.

Feelings are a part of every moment that we experience, therefore, it is important to understand how they work and what the best emotions that we should adopt are, in order to create the life we dreamed of. People are constantly looking for happiness in all sort of things, beyond their own person, while the reality is that happiness lies within us. Happiness is within you and all you have to do is draw from positive feelings that you cultivate. There are seven types of positive and negative feelings;

- *positive feelings*: love, hope, faith, loyalty, enthusiasm, desire,
  aspirations.
- *negative feelings*: fear, jealousy, hatred, malice, revenge,
  superstition, worry.

If you cultivate the positive ones, you'll not only be a happy person, but also a successful and fulfilled one.

Emotions are the result of the emotional states that your mind adopts based on your permission. Each negative emotion may mean enormous losses, if not rejected. Positive emotions are those that offer reasons to live, the needed energy and passion which creates butterflies in your stomach when thinking about future successes. Positive or negative emotions have a remarkable power that, once experienced, manages to rule your life. They have the power to motivate you to go forward when everyone else stops. If controlled, they will lead you to the highest peaks of success, otherwise, you will fail.

To control your emotions means subjecting them to your own values, wisdom, and faith. Not controlling them seriously damages your choices. If negative emotions must be rejected, then the positive ones must be controlled, which means having the discipline that allows you to control them, not vice-versa. Even if you feel like eating in excess, you will limit yourself, because you don't want to want to harm your health. Even if your hormones are going haywire in your body, you will control these emotions, because you don't want to make a costly choice, which will not only violate your morality but also your values. Even if you feel the need to burst and answer back to the person that annoys you, you'll remain positive, or you will respond in an encouraging tone in order to provoke amazement. The purpose of controlling your emotions is not to eliminate them, but instead, the process of ordering them in such a manner that leads to the best choices.

How do emotions influence our choices?

Many people chase happiness in their lives. They have transformed life into a race whose goal is to achieve the grand prize called happiness. Unfortunately, these people will not manage to win this prize, because it doesn't exist. Happiness is not a prize which can be won, but it's a result. The prize in life is life itself.

God gave us this life as a gift, to live it correctly and to enjoy it. Therefore, your goal should be a well-lived life. Happiness is the result of the choices we make. The thing that we choose to focus on will determine whether or not we will be happy. If you focus on every beautiful thing that God has put in you, then you'll be happy. It is not the social status, nor the career or material status which defines a man, but the thoughts which he accepts as reality.

If in your mind, you accept the devil's whispers ("You're not good enough, clever enough!", "You'll never succeed!", "No one loves you!" and so on), then you'll never be happy. These thoughts have no other purpose than making you feel miserable, and your happiness is determined by the way you feel. If you're gripped by positive, energetic and entertaining emotions, then you'll feel very happy, otherwise, you'll feel miserable.

Do you remember the day when you were the happiest person in the world? It was probably the day you met your partner, when your first child was born, when you were accepted to a new job, when you won a medal, helped a person. No matter the event, you've almost certainly experienced something like this. The happiness that you experienced that day was the result of the emotions you felt. What I mean is that emotions are those that determine how happy or miserable we feel, how satisfied or disappointed we are about the life we live.

Our feelings, meaning our emotional state, are triggered by three things we do in every moment:

1) The thoughts on which we focus

Emotions are generated by thoughts, and thoughts are generated by emotions. From each thought that you choose to focus on, influences the way you feel in every moment, and from the way you feel in each moment, comes the way in which you perceive the things around you. Then, in turn, these influence your choices, which are the decisions made in our mind, based on what we've perceived.

Thoughts generate emotions, being the result of the five senses: sight, hearing, smell, taste and touch. The brain receives information through the five senses and forms the thoughts, which then, in turn, transform into perception. The final perception leads to your current emotional state. In other words, the definition we give to experiences, situations, things, is determined by our state. For example, if you find yourself in a boring state of mind, everything around you seems boring. If it's sunny outside and the sun is bright, you'll feel much more energetic than in the case of a cloudy and gloomy sky. Rainy weather affects us as well; that's why we are sleepier and down on such a day.

Anything that reaches our five senses determines our state of mind and this influences our interpretation of certain things. It is for this reason that four people who are looking at the same object interpret it differently. One may find it fun, another may believe it's boring, or an irritant and another may find it interesting. All answers are influenced by the state of mind in which the person finds themselves. The emotions that they feel influence the way they perceive that thing.

I'm sure you've found yourself looking at something, or visiting a particular place and had the impression that it's quite boring, and later experienced a totally different feeling for the same thing. If initially, it seemed a waste of time, now you felt wonderful, but you don't know why. The reason is that the emotional state in which you were was different.

Very often we wonder why people around us cannot see the full cup, or the positive side, like us. In his case, the emotions he has have formed a different state of mind in comparison to our own. It influenced the meaning he gave to things, as well as his perception of them.

A woman had two sons, who opened two different businesses. One of them began a business which involved sandals, and the other one, a business with umbrellas. The mother of these sons was always sad, regardless of the weather. Whether it was rainy or sunny, she was always sad. One day, one of her neighbors decided to ask her why she's sad all the time. The woman answered: "You know, I have two sons and each has a business. When it rains, I'm sad because my son's sandals business doesn't go well. When it's sunny, I'm sad for the other one who owns the business which sells umbrellas. People don't buy umbrellas if the weather is nice, so I can never be happy." The neighbor looked at her and replied excitedly: "You should always be happy because, no matter the weather, your sons always make money. This is a reason for joy. If it rains, the umbrella business goes well, and if it's sunny the sandals business booms. So, one of them always wins!"

The lesson of this illustration is simple: no matter the circumstances, you and I can be happy, if we choose to look on the positive side. The thing we choose to focus on will cause what we feel. For this reason, what really matters isn't the circumstances, but the way our mind perceives them. If the mind perceives something positive, then it generates something positive. Likewise, if it perceives something negative, it will generate something negative. Positivism or negativity causes emotions. If you want to make sure you have control over emotions, then you need to ensure control over your thoughts. If you control your thoughts, you control your emotions. It is important to determine what you see, hear, smell, taste and feel, and not vice-versa.

Usually, most of us are driven by feelings, not the other way around. Let's not forget that from unfiltered information will arise emotional states of mind based on circumstances. In other words, negative and bad moods that we have are nothing else but emotions extracted from information received by our mind. If you want to experience a different life, consider the control of emotions. Your motto in life should be: "I control my emotions, not vice-versa."

Exercise: In order to understand how it works, I suggest this exercise. Try for a day to focus only on positive things. Positively interpret everything you see. Wake up in the morning and tell yourself: "Today is a beautiful day, I feel great, I'm really smart and I'll be a success". Try this and you'll notice that the day will be one of the most productive days that you've ever had, and you'll feel the happiest man on Earth. Forget, for a day, all problems related to home or work, and enjoy a beautiful day. Remember that God gave you the grace to live each day beautifully.

2) The tonality of the voice

God blessed you with a talent called language. In comparison with other talents, it is small, but more powerful than all others, because of the impact that it has on both you, and on the others around you. The Bible describes it as a small limb, which can produce a big fire. Our voice can become either our best friend or our cruelest enemy, depending on the choices we make. The voice can lead to success or failure. What comes first in every communication in the tone of the voice, it determines three things:

• My moods and emotions

The way in which you use your voice gives birth to the emotions that you feel. If I use my voice in an energetic and enthusiastic way, then my emotions and my mood will transform into enthusiastic and energetic feelings. The brain perceives the voice through the auditory sense, interprets and then acts, sending signals to my body, in the following way:

- if we're talking in a stiff voice, it will convey the emotions in the form of rigidity,
- if it perceives passion in the tone adopted, the feelings transmitted will convey passionate ones,
- if it perceives fear and insecurity, it will transmit emotions of fear and insecurity,
- if it perceives words which are full of negativity, it will transmit negative emotions,
- if sensitivity is distinguished, then it will transmit emotions full of tenderness,
- if hustle and anxiety is felt, then it will convey emotions in the form of anxiety and hustle,
- if it perceives happiness and laughter, then it will transmit happy and enjoyable feelings.

To put it simply, your brain is your most faithful friend with which God has endowed you. It will never sabotage you; on the contrary, it will always act on what you left it to believe is beneficial for you, in every moment of your life. If you want to experience positive emotions that will create positive moods, then you have to consciously choose what kind of tonality you adopt at every moment, because it will determine what you will feel.

• Emotions and moods extracted from my entourage

For example, if you are in an entourage in which the people around you speak aggressively, you'll also adopt their tone and will speak aggressively. If you are in an environment where people smile and joke, adopting a tone of good mood and happiness, you will also experience the same emotions, and if you find yourself in a society where the conversation is boring, you will become bored. You can be very enthusiastic and cheerful, but if the mood of the entourage you enter is completely different from yours, sooner or later, their mood will take over.

Not adopting the mood of those around you, means either rejecting the signals received by the brain and replacing them with positive and energetic thoughts, or leaving the circle as soon as possible. In any kind of environment, at some point, sooner or later, you'll adopt the attitude and condition of those who accompany you.

Just think of each conflict that you've had so far, or any exchange of inappropriate words, that you now regret. All of this could have been avoided if you knew the importance of the voice's tone and how it affects your emotions. All you had to do in those moments was to prevent your brain from perceiving the anxiety from the tone of the person with whom you have quarreled, and in no time, you would have experienced reconciliation. No matter how agitated the other person is, if you don't react, and instead transmit calmness with your voice, they will be influenced. Try it for yourself, and next time you experience such a conflict, you will see how much you will gain in the relationship with your partner, children, friends, colleagues, or anyone else.

Most conflicts we've had until now resulted from the tone you've taken during the exchange of words. The words you say have a smaller impact on others than the way you say it. What matters the most is the tone used, because the brain of the person with whom we are talking ' feels' the emotion we have. It's not the joke which makes the difference, but the tone in which it is said which creates emotion for listeners.

In order to inspire confidence and the desire of people to have you around them, they need to know that you are the person that they're searching for, and this will result from the emotions that they experience when talking to you. Whether it's an interview, a contract or a friendly talk, the way you speak determines your success. When you are in front of a person, make sure you're in a state of mind that will positively influence their emotions. People like you or not, depending on the emotions they feel from you, and the good news is that they extract this from the emotions you send through your tonality, meaning the way you talk and through your body language.

- Emotions and moods that you transmit to those around you All of us have friends or favorites. Each of us, instinctively, seeks the company of the hilarious, positive, and overjoyed friend, because we know that in his presence we feel good.

Some people can make something pleasant out of everything, through the way they express themselves. Many believe that the most important thing in communication, in a conversation or in the presentation of a message is the content, when, in fact, what matters most is the manner in which it is issued. The same message can become boring or innovating depending on the tonality and attitude of the person who issues it. Now you understand why your favorite teacher is the one who is playful, excited and who always has a smile on his face. All the same, no matter how cheerful you are, when a teacher comes with a bored and drowsy attitude, you become overwhelmed by his state. The tone of the professor's voice leads to your successfully assimilating that message.

For your message to be received by the one who listens, firstly, it must pass through the person's brain, which establishes if the emotions conveyed are of interest or not. Whether you're a friend, businessman, teacher, parent, or a partner, you must understand that what you send around you, even by a little thing like tonality, matters a lot, because it has the power to decide the mood of those around you.

I encourage you to learn the importance of expressing through the voice and make a decision, starting from today, to spread positivism, happiness, enthusiasm, passion, and love in the lives of the people around. All you have to do is talk differently from how you talked up until now and soon people will want your company more than anything. God created a family for us. We are all part of the same family, called mankind, therefore, each of us should spread love, just as Christ did.

Exercise: In order to make sure you can manage your attitude in every situation, I dare you to try intentionally, several times, the following exercise. In this way, you will transform what you've learned into a belief, which will be stored in the subconscious, and when you find yourself in similar moments, the brain will provide an immediate solution. Look out for clues when you talk to people. Try raising the tone and then lowering it, adopt a high tone, full of energy, then a boring one. In each case, look closely at the reactions of your companions and you will see how they are affected by the tone adopted. Turn your voice into a friend.

3) Body language and facial physiognomy

Body language and facial physiognomy represent the third component that contributes to creating emotions. The physiognomy means facial expression and body language is composed of gestures and posture.

- The expression of my face and my body affects my emotions; if I adopt a boring outfit, I will become bored, if I adopt an interesting one, I will become this way, if I adopt an energetic one, I will become energetic. The outfit transforms feelings, meaning it determines what kind of emotions I experience. If I hold my chest in a vertical position with my shoulders straight, I will feel confident and brave, because, in this way, I tell my brain that I am confident. If I have a dull face, shoulders down, bent back, I will feel bored and tired, because I suggest to myself that I don't have enough energy. If I put a smile on my face, although I'm very sad, I will experience feelings of happiness and I'm going to feel positive. If you are really bored but adopt an energetic posture, you will feel energetic, because your brain will send such emotions.

Just think that all you feel is influenced by the attitude you adopt. Adopt an attitude of fear and you will feel fear; adopt an attitude of stress and you will feel stressed out. If until now you've felt what you did it is because, without realizing, you have sent to the brain the signals in question. You and I have the power to influence our emotional moods, so, if it happens and you have a bad day, remember that it's due to you, and if you have a nice day it's all thanks to you. God gave you everything you need to transform each day into a pleasant memory. Imagine, what your life would look like, if at the end of each day, you could say, "God, thanks for the wonderful day I had with you!", wouldn't this be great? You can do this if you understand the importance of the attitude you adopt.

- My facial and body expression affect the emotions of those around me

Not only you, can experience a marvelous life, but also those around you because your physiognomy and tonality of the voice create emotions on others.

For example, the smile that you display may create positive emotions in the people you meet. All of us spread emotions, and the good news is that we decide what kind of emotions. We can spread happiness, energy, enthusiasm, smiles, or, on the contrary, stress, worry, anxiety, fear. Choose to be the person who transmits positive emotions, wherever you are. Through your attitude, you can either transmit a crumb of God's kindness, or the bitter taste of the devil.

You also can contribute to something in people's lives, even if you will never meet them. A passing smile can change someone's day; a nice gesture can change someone's emotional state. Choose a positive attitude, if you want to positively inspire others.

• Facial and body expressions of those around us affects emotions

Did you ever happen to be part of an entourage in which people yawned and had bored or tired faces? It has happened to me several times, and I guess to you too. What I was able to observe is that, in those situations, no matter how energetic I was, after just a few minutes spent in their presence, I became like them. I began yawning and adopting a dull and boring posture. Through the help of my eyes, the brain has informed me of everybody's moods and forwarded me a similar state of mind.

The brain is the one that determines each emotion you feel, according to the information received. If it perceives a state of boredom and fatigue, it will transfer it to you. If you don't reject it intentionally, you will end up bored and tired, although before you had a different mood. With each person you meet and from every place you go, in every moment, you assimilate information and based on this, the brain creates emotions.

If you work in an environment where people are stressed out, sooner or later, you'll also become stressed. If you work in a place where people are happy, funny, and energetic, you will become the same. If you work in a place where the individuals are negative, but you don't want to let yourself get affected by their moods, you have only two alternatives: either look for another job or influence yourself and your emotions, by the attitude that you adopt, in spite of the environment. You have the power to decide what your brain assimilates, through the adoption of a physiognomy, a mental and a positive tonality.

Most of us live our life based on circumstances. If the nature of them is positive, then I will have a positive attitude, if these are disappointing and painful, then I will be the same. Do not let circumstances influence the most precious gift that God gave you, namely your life. You either choose what you feel in every situation, or the situations will determine how you feel. Choose instead to influence your circumstances, through the attitude that you adopt. Choose what emotions and moods you want to have. Choose, regardless of the environment in which you enter, regardless of the mood of those around you, to continue focusing on healthy thoughts, adopting a positive attitude, full of enthusiasm, passion, and energy.

If you do these things, you'll become immune to the circles in which you enter, and even better, you will be able to influence others with your own energetic, positive, and fun mood.

Our emotions and moods decide what we see. We see the full or the empty glass, depending on the state of mind we find ourselves in. A cheerful state of mind brings along rewards such as positivism, creativity, and profitable choices, therefore, you'll experience what you focus on, because choices lead to action, and actions lead to experiences.

Why is it important to know these things? Because they have an influence on our choices. You can be the best and have the best beliefs about your partner or anyone else, but nevertheless, the present mood will manipulate your beliefs. You can have the best habits, which is important, but at the same time, forget about your emotional state.

My encouragement to you is to not let anyone influence your mood because they will influence your later choices and you'll regret it. If you fall into a bad mood, quickly seek to change it, as soon as you notice it. Don't let it spoil your day. You and only you are responsible for your choices and emotions. Control them!

How to control your emotions and get rid of depression

Depression is an unconscious choice, which you make yourself. You are the one who lets depression rule you. In order for a person to become depressed, all he needs to do is to accept that negative voice through which the devil is trying to convince the mind of all negative things whispered repeatedly, such as: "You are worth nothing!", "You are insignificant!"," You'll never succeed!", "No one loves you!"," You don't look good enough!", "You'll end up bankrupt!"... and the list goes on.

All these whispers that you hear in your mind will take control of your emotions, and from that moment on, your sentimental state will change and you will end up in depression. The easiest way to get rid of depression is to ensure that you do not accept it. Depression results from negative thoughts which bombard you. If you accept and focus on them, it will influence your emotions, and the emotions will affect your emotional state of mind. To avoid falling into depression, you must pay attention to the following things:

1) Emotions – In order to control emotions and present moods, you have to be able to identify them, when they occur. Once the indisposition, fear or grief tries to make room and control you, you must realize that it is harmful and that it will affect you. Once you acknowledge this, you will be able to make the next step.

2) Focus – You must never stay focused on negative emotions after you've identified them because they will influence your emotional state and you'll fall into depression. If you've identified these emotions, in the next second, you must redirect your attention onto something else, preferably something extremely positive and enthusiastic. Think about a moment in your life that brings you great pleasure and positivism, and when the ailment comes, change your attention from the negative arguments, which provoke that emotional state, to positive experiences that have helped you stay in the past. Everything is done in fractions of a second, so you need to take control and drive your emotions, not vice-versa.

Depression is the result of negative experiences which a person had in the past. If you're in a depression, it is due to the fact that you let yourself be controlled by negative feeling. What you need to do is get rid of those emotions by taking control and changing your focus from negative to positive.

3) Alternatives – No matter how depressed a person may be, he can escape from depression when he creates alternatives to the emotions that controlled his life and to the choices he made so far. All you have to do is to change the focus of the emotions. You either control them, or they will control you. How do you create alternatives? Well, by changing your beliefs about the past, about you, about others, about any negative experiences that you have gone through.

Typically, depression is associated with negative emotions created through the interpretation of some unpleasant or painful events from the past, which have affected and continue to affect your life continuously, until today. To get rid of those negative moods, you need to replace them with other positive ones, to shift your focus. Each emotion that you experience can either be negative or positive. Look at the purpose of the emotion in question, in order to understand and redirect it, or to get rid of it as fast as possible. Ask yourself what kind of feelings they cause, good or bad, and if they aren't for your strengthening, instantly eliminate them, because otherwise, they will continue to affect your choices and beliefs. By applying this method, you'll discover that, behind the emotion lies one of the two strengths, the devil or the Holy Spirit. Choose to be guided by the Holy Spirit and you will live a flawless life, a positive and prosperous one, together with God.

Finally, depression is nothing more than the devil's method of manipulating people, making them feel miserable, believing that they are unskilled, insignificant, or without value. If you are struggling with these things, you have to understand that these are nothing more than lies which are unrelated to you. You're not what he or she believes about you, but you are what you believe about yourself. God calls you His art. Choose to accept God's image of you and to reject everything others believe you to be. The only way for you to be what you are is not to be as they are. Be fully satisfied with what you are and acknowledge that they will never be what you are. This means that you should be proud of the person you are.

In conclusion, you should know three things:

a) Depression is a conscious choice that I make, every time I decide to focus on negative thoughts, on a negative tone and a negative physiognomy.

b) Depression can be eliminated forever if I consciously choose to focus on positive thoughts, if I choose a positive tone and a positive physiognomy.

I choose an energetic, positive, fun attitude, instead of depression, knowing that this is nothing more than the choice to focus on what God says you are. Otherwise, you'll have to agree with what the devil whispers to you. God created you in his own light, so spread it by living an exemplary life.

5

Habits

When a thing is done repeatedly, again and again, it becomes a custom, meaning a habit. Habits that we cultivate influence our decision making regarding the future. It is crucial to understand that what you usually do and how you do it will become beliefs that you will adopt. It's like with a weighing scale: the pan on which you put more weight will determine the inclination. If you constantly cultivate, enhance, and seed a bad habit, the pan will bend in its favor; the same happens when you cultivate and put emphasis on a positive and beneficial habit.

If you have convinced yourself that the habit of being late isn't so bad, then you will become a delayed person; if you have convinced yourself that alcohol is good, then you will become an alcoholic; if you have convinced yourself that smoking is not so bad, then you will become a smoker; if you have convinced yourself that drugs aren't so harmful, then you will become a junkie; if you have convinced yourself that stealing is not so bad, then you will become a thief; if you have convinced yourself that people are bad, then you will become an egocentric; if you have convinced yourself that God does not exist, then you will become an atheist; if you have convinced yourself that morality does not exist, then you will become an immoral man; if you have convinced yourself that you are an accident, then your life will be lived by accident.

The question you have to ask yourself is, "What habits have I cultivated and how will these affect me?" Each of us constantly decides how we approach the things around us, but what we need to know is that we make many of these choices due to cultivated habits that have been influenced by our beliefs. Have you ever wondered why you don't manage to change, although you know that you need to change? Well, as long as you continue with the same routine, habits, it is impossible to get a different result. The result will change, but first, you need to change your habits.

For example, many people continue to eat poorly, believing that the pill they take will do wonders and that overnight they will have an ideal body. This is a lie that they sell to themselves and that does not bring any change. Want a different body? Then you have to cultivate different habits. Set in mind to eat healthy, to sleep properly and train your body. Act in this manner and the result will be different. Negative habits will lead to negative results, and positive ones will bring positive results. What you breed, that you shall reap. If you cultivate good habits in your daily routine, then these will lead you to success. You must decide what you want to do with your life and how you want to live it. If you want to live it by chance, then the habits you currently have don't really matter, but if you have decided you want to do something meaningful, then you have to set goals.

Once you have a plan for your life, the next step is cultivating positive habits. To become a successful person, you need to think, speak, believe, choose, and act as a successful person. You can't just stand and wait, hoping that someday God will have mercy on you and transform you overnight into a successful person. He gave you all you need to become that person, and now it's your turn to redirect what you have received, towards success. After you verify the habits, both the good and bad ones, you have to start the transformation process. Habits are of two kinds: good and bad. Both categories affect us according to their nature. Good habits are positive and beneficial because they reflect our personality, but these are not sufficient. Most of us settle on good habits, forgetting that there are much better ones.

Once, a wise man asked a teenager what kind of habits he thought he had. The teenager immediately replied: "Good ones, Sir!" The wise man advised him: "You should be careful with those good habits that you have because it will limit the cultivation of others which are much better ". The teenager was speechless, not realizing that the man was right. The majority of us have just good habits; this is why mediocrity is our society's standard. Many settle on being a good person with good values and habits. On the other hand, very good habits are composed of a person's aspirations, with very good values, and with great beliefs. These habits not only ensure a better life but motivate us to create a better life for those around us. Most of us are grateful if we are in a good position, but people who have very good habits focus on creating good for those around them. It is not enough just to have a relationship with God, but I want those around me to have such a relationship.

6

Addictions

Addictions are habits which you have lost control of, which created addiction, obsession, or a sense of the loss of control. The addiction is a compulsive habit, which surpassed the stage of choice: a psychic and physical attachment to a particular thing, which, when withdrawn, causes retreat or intensification of symptoms. Whether they are positive or negative habits, they influence the choices we make. Anything in life, regardless of its nature, once used in excess can provoke obsession and become an addiction.

Addictions are wrong, regardless of their nature, because it negatively influences choices. When you're driven by addictions, you consciously choose to practice certain habits, although you're convinced that it causes you harm, or that they are inappropriate and unethical. Addictions can arise from good habits, moral and positive or from bad habits, immoral and negative.

Addictions originating from positive habits
Each individual has a set of good habits that he practices in life and that are important, beneficial, leading to a positive result. But, if at some point, they get out of control, these can cause damage to the life of the individual in question. I will give some simple examples, upon which you can reflect:

food, sleep, sex, job... and the list continues. Think about what will happen to the person who is eating excessively, making this good and vital habit for the body, an exaggeration. The consequences will be disastrous: fattening, high cholesterol, diabetes, hormonal deregulation of the metabolism and others. So, here's how a good habit becomes harmful and destructive if it's exaggerated.

Imagine a person who gradually becomes obsessed with sleeping. What will happen to him? Not only will he become irresponsible and lazy, but over time, he will cause damage to the body because of over-sleeping slows down the brain activity. It no longer functions optimally; every choice is affected and, as a result, his life is affected. The same pattern is true in everything in life that, although positive, once exaggerated, quickly gets out of control and produces a disaster, influencing choices in a significant and destructive manner.

"First we form habits, then they form us. Defeat your bad habits or else you will be defeated by them." (Rob Gilbert)

Addiction arising from negative habits

Good habits are important and we need them to function, but only as long as they are positive, moral, and help our growth in any form. Once they become wrong, negative and pull us down, harming our health, morality, and values, they are destructive. Maybe they don't harm your values, but nevertheless, they pull you down and don't allow you to grow.

If this happens, you have to get rid of them immediately, otherwise, they'll transform into addictions and will cause even more harm. Things that have become addictions, will make your life miserable or even destroy you. Seek to be very careful with the habits you cultivate and release yourself from the negative and immoral ones, starting from the stage when they're just habits. Under no circumstance, should you let them pass this first stage.

There are many people who for some reason were not aware of the negative effects that the habits may have over their lives. Some, because of a suffering they have experienced, resorted to certain harmful habits related to overcoming that problem: drugs, alcohol, tobacco etc.

Others, because of the curiosity of trying something new, have picked up a habit that managed to control his life. Regardless of the way in which they adopted certain habits, what is certain is that they have to get rid of them immediately so that they can be in control of their life and function properly. You also want to function correctly and make the best choices, because you want wonderful experiences of fulfillment, happiness, love, health, prosperity and influence.

Find a way to keep your balance at all times in life, so that you can choose wisely and experience a very good life. Any positive or negative habits which get out of control become an addiction. By their very nature, addictions are harmful and destructive, therefore avoid extremes. A wonderful life will always come as a result of balance, but an addiction will go against your beliefs and will influence you, because it is manipulated by the devil, through carnal lusts and desires. There are so many people that live by breaking God's moral nature continuously but who seek change, but they can't seem to find the necessary power to do so.

In the next section of the book, I will help you escape from any addiction, regardless of its nature, set free from the enemy's power. Life is beautiful if you know how to live it beautifully. Keep a smooth balance of moral things, completely reject everything that is immoral and you'll live beautifully.

7

Change

Change, for some, is a fear from which they constantly run and for others, it is the component used to achieve success. If you're a person who associates change with something negative, then you must get rid of this belief, because it deprives you of all the beautiful moments you could experience once the change is made. Many people prefer the comfort zone instead of change because they did things in their own way their whole life. In other words, they feel uneasy and experience a sense of discomfort regarding the change. However, the real change is nothing but improvement.

In these times, the world in which we live, together with the society is subject to constant change. Things change on a daily basis with incredible speed, therefore, the one who does not keep up with society in order to adapt to change will soon experience what I call, a blockage. It's the moment when someone feels surpassed by everything around them because he does not live in the present time. If you also have problems adapting to society, then you have to change and relate differently to it. People who feel overwhelmed try to live today as yesterday, but this kind of behavior always brings frustrations and disappointments. In no circumstances is today like yesterday and vice versa. In other words, you cannot apply yesterday's methods to today, because they have changed.

Perhaps you've thought about what change means and keeping up with society. Does this imply you need to go over your values, character, and principles? The answer is no. All of these are essential components of your character and it is a good thing to keep them, but what you need to change are your methods. While on Earth, Jesus constantly changed its methods, but not the message. The message is the same, but the way you present it changes depending on society, culture, and the era in which you live. If you really want to experience a change in your relationship with your partner, children, those around you, then you have to change, because the way you relate to them will make a difference. If you want to experience a change in the business you run, then you must change first. The change that a business will experience will come only as a result of the transformation of the person who runs it.

When change becomes a necessity, the first thing that should be changed is me. This is you. If you want to constantly increase your success, then you must change constantly. There is almost certainly one thing in your life that ought to be changed or that you decided to change but haven't taken any steps in this direction yet. Maybe you thought you should get rid of that habit or addiction, maybe it's a belief that limits you and you want to eliminate, it or maybe it's depression that destroys your happiness. Whatever change you need, I will help you achieve it. Change means growth, success, achievement.

Why don't we change?

We know that our life is affected by our daily decisions and we even know the things which influence our choices. However, we continue to choose wrongly and irresponsibly. The secret to a different life lies in making different choices, but in order to do so, we must change our limited thinking. This means paying attention to the beliefs that have a negative influence, to our curiosities, and being capable of controlling our emotions, to change our unfavorable habits which pull us down and, last but not least, to eliminate our addictions.

In order to choose differently, we must change everything which is not beneficial to the five influences. However, an issue is encountered whenever we want to change something in our lives, and the problem is the lack of desire, will, or fear. This is due to the negative beliefs of the person who does not believe, who is afraid, who rejects or denies change. Most of us do not accept transformation because we have convinced ourselves that this is not a priority, or we simply don't want to change because we can't manage to change ourselves. The list below represents some of the reasons why we fail to change:

- we believe that we don't need a change,
- we believe that a change it is not that important
- we believe that we cannot change ourselves
- we believe that change means pain, suffering, or torture
- we believe that change means loss
- we believe change means unfulfillment, unhappiness, and dissatisfaction

From the list that I've presented, what is the belief behind the failure to change? Is it the fact that you don't need a change? If yes, then you've either got used to the life and choices you're currently experiencing, or you've just used your subconscious, to lie to yourself that you're okay. If you're going to be honest with yourself, you'll realize that no matter how good, or bad you choose, there will always be things you have to change or develop.

Change is of two kinds:

- *revolutionary* – involves a radical change, from the smallest to the most significant things;
- *evolutionary* – involves improvement and development, of choices, customs, or beliefs.

Discover which of the two you need to apply. Any kind of positive change will bring growth in your life. In discovering the need to change, you have to use both your logic and beliefs, in order to verify if what you believe is what you see. You may believe that change is not important when you look through the beliefs point of view, but when you look at it in terms of logic and reality, you'll discover a whole new truth. If what you perceive is not what you experience as a result of your choices, then you should think more deeply about this. God gave you the gift of choice through which you can guide your life. It lies in your hands, so use it wisely.

Opposing to the concept of change is universal and influences all classes and individuals. Each generation before us experienced this opposition. No matter what you think about change, what you have to understand is that if you do not accept it, you will stop progressing and will continue to choose at the expense of your health, body, relationships, resources, etc.

Different choices are due to different beliefs. As long as you think that your habits are beneficial, you won't have the power to change them.

If you have convinced yourself that you lack potential, you won't succeed, you won't be able to make a difference, you won't have an impact and influence and you won't change, no matter how much I tell you that you can. A person's beliefs affect his choices. Whatever you think about the things or people around they will significantly affect your life, because these thoughts influence your choices. Once your brain receives images, positive or negative, about what change means, it will take action based on those images, creating beliefs that will determine how you will respond to change.

Below are four steps that you need to take to change a habit or a belief, or to eliminate an addiction. For any kind of change, in any area of life, whether we are talking about choices, beliefs, thoughts, habits, addictions, feelings, etc., we need four things, without which any kind of change is not possible. These four things prepare the ground for change. They liberate the path so that change takes. It's just like those official columns that liberate the road in order for the president to pass without being hindered or blocked by any obstacles.

1) Identification – "I should change!"
When a habit, belief, feeling, thought or addiction doesn't create fulfillment and satisfaction, you'll immediately observe this and think: "I think I

should do something about this." Such a decision opens our eyes towards the reality of the things that need to be changed. You meditate upon it for a time and somewhere inside, you know you should go ahead and change. But you won't succeed as long as you stay at the stage of "I ought to" because this doesn't represent an immediate interest in taking action.

I hear daily, and you probably do too, people who constantly tell themselves that they should do something in a certain area, but never get around to action. They know that those habits that they've cultivated must be changed, but they never find the necessary motivation to do anything in this respect. Perhaps you are in this situation. The question that you must address to yourself is, "why?" The answer is simple: that habit does not represent a priority for you, because you seem to have a connection with something far away, in the future.

You know people who say: "I should do something to save money, I should do something with my relationship, I should begin a diet, I should eat healthier, I should work out..."? The term "should" will not produce the necessary change, because this doesn't represent a priority or motivation. The question is "Then what should I do to change?" Always start with identifying the things you want to change, but don't stop here, continue the process. This is just the first step, and now it's time to move forward to the next level.

2) *Desire* – "I want to change!"

After discovering the things that should be changed, we must go further and solemnly decide in our hearts that we want to change. One of the main reasons people don't change is that they don't want it badly enough, either because they feel well in the present, or because they experience a sense of power and influence.

Some of us know that we should change the way we talk or the aggressive behavior used to intimidate people. However, we don't want to do this, because we feel important. We know we should renounce these addictions or habits, but because we feel good at the moment, we don't accept transformation, although long-term results are disastrous.

For example, you know that you should not cheat on your wife, being conscious that you'll destroy your marriage, children, and reputation, but because you feel good at the moment, you don't want to give this habit up. You know you shouldn't yell because it's a horrible habit, but because it provides a sense of power over your children, wife, or employees, you prefer to keep it. You know you shouldn't smoke because you're aware that it's not beneficial for your health and it consumes your financial resources, but still, you're not willing to give in because you feel good at the moment. You know it's not ok to be late or to gossip others, but because you receive attention from those who listen, you keep on doing it. In order to achieve change, you must commit 100% and convince yourself that you want to change. You need to pick change, otherwise, it will be impossible to change something. "I want to change!" is the second step.

3) Necessity – "I have to change!"
After identifying the habit or any other thing that you want to change, the confirmation comes, meaning the need: "I must change, I am forced and compelled to do something in this direction because this thing prevents me from evolving". You become convinced not only that you should and want to change something, but also that it is an emergency. Now, here, right in this moment, you need to get started.

Pay attention to an excuse that we often invoke in order to prevent change: "I know that I must change something, but I want to be helped by him or her... ". Maybe you're thinking of a psychologist or a therapist that can help you. When you invoke this excuse, you are releasing yourself from the responsibility of assuming change. All of these people can lend a helping hand, but only you can become responsible and accept reality. Real change can only be achieved by you. I can help you by explaining the steps you need to follow, but I will never be capable of changing you. This process is up to you, therefore, repeat to yourself: "I have to change".

Now, I'll present the steps that will help you achieve change, but don't forget that you are the one who has to make it. Therefore, the "I have to change" is the third step that reflects the need for a change.

4) Ability – "I believe I can change!"

The fourth and final step, after you have identified the habit you want to change and understood that this is an urgent need, is to believe that you can. Why is it important what I think? Have you ever seen someone who makes efforts and invests in something they don't believe in? Nobody devotes time, effort, resources and energy into something they don't believe. In order to really change, you have to believe you can. "I know I need to, but I can't!" Most people find all sorts of excuses to justify failure: "I've tried everything, or I tried in every way, in thousands of ways!" and thus we begin to lie to ourselves.

One of the reasons we believe these lies so easily is that we've never experienced a change in that area before. Once you have convinced your brain that it is impossible to change, it will be impossible. Why?

Because at that point you have offered a definition, a negative image which has been assimilated, and now, that image will lead you feelings. The belief will prevent you from continuing to seek for solutions. In this way, you will be blocked and make the same wrong choices that will lead to the same unsatisfying or even harmful consequences.

The brain continually gathers information in relation to a certain thing, until the moment you take a positive or negative decision regarding what you think about that thing. At that point, you find a definition which is taken up by the brain and transformed into neural connections in the form of a belief.

Therefore, never think that a habit cannot be removed or changed because, the moment you have implemented this idea, your brain will stop processing and searching for solutions. If, however, you don't rush to draw a conclusion, the brain will continue to process, and finally, through its extraordinary ability, will find the solution. You have to think you can, even if you haven't succeeded yet. Maybe the method you tried was not the best, maybe the environment or your approach have stopped you, but no matter what you've tried, you have to believe it is possible.

Another reason you didn't succeed until now is that you've convinced yourself that you did all you could, which is a lie, or that it is impossible to succeed, which again is a lie. The reality is that we live in a world full of negative people, who ensure you that you won't succeed, but you have to get beyond what they tell you. Seek to replace the belief you have about the thing you wish to change and think that you can. Then, nothing will be able to stop you, and change will come easily.

These four beliefs are not change itself, but determine the success or failure of the change process. In order for change to occur, you need to make sure that nothing stands in the way. Any obstacle can prevent us from experiencing it.

In conclusion, how do I change something? First, I need to identify that particular thing, then confirm it, meaning understanding that there is a need to change it now, today. The third step is to believe that I have to change it, taking as a reference point the reality that I currently experience, not the illusion that I am now convinced I don't want. The last step is to destroy the belief which I've formed about a certain thing and be sure that I can change it.

All steps are related to beliefs. If you've managed to convince yourself that it's not so bad, then you won't be motivated to change, but once you have come to the conclusion that you have to do it, you'll take action, and motivation will occur. Everything you want to change in your life starts with beliefs that can either stop you or motivate you on your way to changing. Beliefs motivate but also bring limitation. Used correctly, they will propel you, used wrongly, they will bring limitations.

How do I change my beliefs?

In order to embrace change and do something in this respect, you have to convince yourself that change is worth fighting for. All negative images and beliefs that you have about what change means, have to be replaced with other positive and motivating ones, which will lead to different and positive choices. There are two steps that, once followed, will allow you to reach the four beliefs which will ease your way to change:

1) The first step is to associate change with something positive, urgent, necessary, and beneficial. Identify from these six beliefs the ones that you have and change them, one after another. In order for the process to be simple, I suggest you use a sheet of paper, because later on, these will have to be repeated constantly until the positive ones replace the negative ones.

Example: "I can't change" must transform into "I can change", or "it is not important to change" into "it is very important to me", or "I don't need a change" into "I need a change".

Once you believe that change means something necessary, positive, and urgent, you will find the necessary motivation and opening you need to make this step. The secret is to replace every negative belief with a positive one. Attention! All beliefs must be identified and replaced. In this way, the road will be cleared up and you will be free to move forward. If you have not managed to identify all of them, then the result will not be 100% positive.

2) The second step is to associate the lack of change with pain, suffering and with immediate and massive loss. When you understand that stagnation causes pain and loss, you'll more easily replace this belief, although at first, it will oppose resistance. The more you repeat this idea and visualize the loss and believe that you will suffer if you don't change, the more the negative belief will turn into a positive one.

Example: The lack of change means suffering, loss, and grief.

Your brain doesn't want you to change because it has received clear information from you that you're ok as you are, or that you don't need a change. But now, all the information that you have turned into beliefs should be replaced step by step, in order for your brain to allow and help you to change. Prepare two lists: one with the benefits that change will bring, and the other with losses that you will have if you continue in the same way. Read them daily for several days, until what you thought before is no longer what you think now. In other words, read them until you open up to change and accept its process in the areas about which I wrote earlier.

After you have made the first step, things will flow naturally. Beliefs must be positive and in line with the four beliefs: I should, I must, I want to change, and then change is 100% possible.

Actual change

Firstly, change is mostly defined by the four beliefs outlined above, but these are just the first step. Beliefs are important because they free the path to change. But now we need a second step, through which we accomplish change. Before you proceed to the actual change, make sure you have found what you should change, what you want to change, what needs to change and what you believe you can change. Now, when the path is clear, it's time to get down to work. Identify the habit or addiction you want to change and begin the change process.

1) Motivation

The reason for not changing, although you are aware that changes must be made, is that you don't have the necessary motivation to produce that change.

You have changed that negative belief about change, you believe you should change using the four beliefs, but now you face opposition because your brain doesn't successfully assimilate the idea of change. What should you do? The answer is that you need to create enough motivation. The mistake we often make is not being realistic in what we want to change. Somehow, you've lied, convincing yourself that it's not really that bad, and thus, because you've slightly sweetened the idea of change, you find yourself lacking motivation.

Example: You want to quit that cigarette that destroys your health, body, economies, but, at the same time you said to yourself: "I love to smoke" or "I can't cope without smoking". All of this will prevent your change. Why? Because you're not 100% motivated. On the one hand, you want it, but on the other, you don't want it because it makes you feel good.

Another example: You want to lose weight and be in shape, healthy and good looking, but at the same time, you're not convinced that this is a problem if you're a little fat, have high cholesterol and don't have the ideal shape. The motivation to change does not exist. Why? Because you're not 100% convinced that you desire that change. "To want" is not the same as "To have to", just like "I would change" is not the same as "I will change".

The first thing I ask those who say they would give up or would change is "Do you want it or not?" To desire is not enough to convince me that you want it. The reality is that most don't really want to renounce current habits because of wrongful beliefs, through which they have lied to themselves. Change is possible, feasible and guaranteed, but only when you have the correct motivation. If you have not managed to change yet, then maybe you have a wrong image about what change implies. You're miserable, unhappy, and unfulfilled because you want to eliminate certain thing but, at the same time, you believe that change might mean pain or suffering. In this way, your brain will avoid change. Why? Because it doesn't want you to suffer. You want to change, but you're afraid of failure. In this situation, the disappointment of a possible failure will be huge, and the brain will avoid change because it associates it with fear, disappointment of a potential loss.

You want to change, but you're afraid that you will not succeed. In this situation, the disappointment of a possible failure will be even greater, and the brain will omit the change, because it is associated with fear, with disappointment or a potential loss. Look at the thing that you want to change and verify your beliefs. What's your opinion about it?

Example of an addiction: Smoking

Answer the below questions by which you will bring to the surface the beliefs you possess, both positive and negative.

Positive beliefs: Why do I want to change? What benefit will change bring? How can I use those benefits? Will I be fulfilled, happy, and satisfied? What can I do with the saved money, if I change? What is the next investment that I have in mind, but I don't have enough money for, and how could I use the money saved from cigarettes to invest in that thing?

Negative beliefs: Why don't I desire to change? What benefits do I have as a result of smoking? How does smoking affect me physically, psychologically, economically, materially, financially? Am I fulfilled, happy, and satisfied in the long run, or just for the present moment, and do

I hate what I do afterward? How much money do I spend on cigarettes, money that I could save and invest in my dreams, desires, relationships, or in anything else? How does it affect my health?

If you've answered both to the positive and the negative questions, you will have two different lists, with positive and negative beliefs about the thing you want to eliminate. The next step is to write another list of all good beliefs that you have about smoking, but which in fact are negative. For example I like smoking because it makes me feel good, I like smoking because it makes me feel important, I like smoking because it calms me down, I like smoking because it reduces my stress levels... Whatever the reasons, you have to identify them, in order to eliminate them and move on.

It is absolutely necessary to change the place of the beliefs, meaning to move the good ones to the negative list and vice versa.

For example:

- If you wrote: "I like to smoke because it reduces my stress level", now you must write: "I hate to smoke because it stresses me out";
- If you wrote: "I like to smoke because I feel important", now write: "I hate to smoke because it makes me miserable and unimportant";
- If you wrote: "I can't give up smoking", now write: "I can give up smoking";
- If you wrote: "I don't want to give up smoking," now write: "I want to give up smoking."

Example of a habit: Being late

Answer the below questions by which you bring to the surface your beliefs, both positive and negative.

Positive beliefs: Why do I want to change? Why do I want to be a punctual person? How would my image improve if I became punctual? How will others appreciate me? How will I feel? Will I become a responsible person?

Negative beliefs: Why don't I change? What do I have to lose if I change? How will others perceive me if I don't change? How much time will I lose if I always go over the established program? How will my image suffer, if I continue to be a delayed person?

After you've answered the questions above, you will obtain two different lists, one with positive things and another with negative things. Changing their place, you'll get enough negative reasons to figure out how you will be affected if you don't change and enough positive reasons to make that change.

You must do the same with each addiction and habit. You need to convince yourself that it is compulsory to renounce these habits because they produce suffering, pain, bitterness and because you hate it. By reaching this conclusion and changing your beliefs, you'll have all the needed motivation to accept the transformation.

When you convince your brain that if you don't change you'll suffer, then you'll change, but if you believe that change provokes pain, you will never change, because you do not have enough reasons to cause change. We have the ability to manipulate ourselves and force ourselves to change. If the present is painful, we can always create an alternative future.

In order to experience a change, you need to be honest with yourself, "Yes, I need this change now, so I'll begin to change something in the present", otherwise, the future will be the same, no matter how much you try to imagine it differently. You have to motivate your brain to change because it sends you signals and you have to win the fight with it.

How to produce motivation in order to achieve change?

A. Negative association
Lack of change must be associated in your mind with negative effects resulting from sorrow, suffering and massive and immediate, profound loss. These are the keywords. Why don't you quit smoking, drugs, unhealthy food, being late, losing time on insignificant things, using nasty

words, aggression, gossip, judgmental thinking, yelling? (All of these and many others are negative and must be changed.) Because you did not understand that they are destructive and unhealthy. Recognize them, put them in the present tense, and then you'll be motivated to change. Don't "send" them into the future ("I'll get cancer", "I get fat" and "I will destroy my health," etc.), because then you won't find it necessary to change. The problem with "I will" is that it eliminates the urgency and creates the illusion that it will be good... someday.

B. Positive association

You need to associate the change in your mind with its positive effects: earning income, satisfaction, fulfillment, massive and immediate, deep happiness. We humans don't change just because a particular thing affects us, but when we understand the effects and benefits of change. Change has no connection with our ability, but with our motivation. Ability will come along with motivation. When someone has enough reasons, they will undoubtedly change.

Were you ever in a critical situation where you had to do something that you thought it was impossible? This is called motivation. Need leads you toward anything, but you have to be sufficiently motivated.

2) Destabilizing the belief

Once you have found the required motivation for change, you are on the path to that change, but there is one thing that needs to be done to ensure reliable results. It is called belief destabilization. So far, you have accumulated a certain set of beliefs about what a certain thing means to you and why you're doing it. For example, maybe you smoke because you love it because you don't think you can change, or because smoking reduces stress.

What does this example mean? It outlines the fact that wrong beliefs exist, by which you reassure yourself of the impossibility or unwillingness to produce a change. Somewhere inside, you know you should, but you will never succeed until you get rid of the beliefs that stop you. In other words, a pattern has formed and you need to eliminate it. The belief is the image that you've formed about a particular thing, based on information received from the brain. In order for the image to be transformed into a belief, some information about that thing is needed, from which a conclusion can be drawn, positive or negative.

Imagine belief or faith in the form of a comfortable chair on which you're sitting. The legs support the seat, but once cut, it destabilizes the seat. Each leg represents an informative image, which sustains the belief. For example, if I were to ask you a question, "Why do you believe stealing is wrong?" you'll give me a couple of reasons which support this if you're really convinced. You can tell me that stealing is wrong because you deceive people, or because you cause damage to someone, or because it shows poor morality, or because it produces suffering for the robbed person... and the list can continue.

What I want to emphasize is that the reasons you present to me are the "legs" which stabilize the belief. If the belief is good, the results are impressive and produce something positive. Unfortunately, it is the same with harmful beliefs.

Somehow, you have put up the wrong "legs", which sustain wrong beliefs. These must be eliminated, replacing them with other beliefs which are sustained by other "legs". Still, a belief cannot be eliminated just because you have an argument against it. No!

First of all, it is necessary for the old "legs" to be removed and replaced with new ones, which are true and positive, which allow you to change the seat. Once the old chair no longer has legs, it falls to the ground and collapses, and you're forced to create another one.

- Identification – the first step is to find every "leg" which supports the belief that you want to change. Attention! The chair may have three or ten "legs", and the belief will still exist if it has enough "legs"; which is why it is mandatory to identify all of them. If you remove only a few of them, the belief will resist. You'll still "sit" on that belief, although it is no longer as safe and stable. However, what you seek is to eliminate it immediately after you destabilize it. The images behind it differ from situation to situation. It can be a belief sustained by three, four, or more arguments. The most important thing is that they are eliminated.

- Destabilization – the second step is to loosen the "legs", meaning the images that lay behind the belief.

Each of us has information that strengthens the adopted position. These are the images that must be weakened so that we can slowly destabilize and afterward, eliminate them. To do this, it is best to ask ourselves a challenging question, for example: "What if my position is not the best?" I can be convinced that smoking reduces stress that it makes me seem important and I can't give it up. But what if these are just manipulated arguments which prevent us from succeeding? Whatever they are, they represent a "leg" which supports the belief, that's why they must be discredited.

- Elimination – after you have identified all of them, try eliminating them one by one. Attention! Elimination is not possible without the fourth step, namely:
- Replacement – the purpose of the brain is to provide the body with a smooth functioning and, for this reason, it opposes the process of eliminating the wrong beliefs, seeking to avoid suffering and preserve comfort. So, what you need to do at this point is to immediately replace each "leg" with another. By doing this, you give the brain a sense of safety, creating the illusion that a "leg" is still there when in fact, it is another. Substituting each negative image ("leg") with a positive one will allow, the brain to give in and allow the "seat'" replacement, with one of your choices.

I advise you to also use the tactic of replacement, not just elimination, in order to achieve a positive effect in the future. It is obvious that in order to quit smoking, you must eliminate cigarettes. This is achievable if you have made a plan for the future, in which you more wisely use the money you previously wasted on cigarettes.

You can eliminate this addiction, but you have to be careful because the money earned now can be wasted on other unimportant things, if you don't invest it in an intelligent and beneficial way. The same happens if you've decided to quit eating unhealthy food and drinking poor beverages. Once you have replaced the beliefs which supported this habit and you are now convinced that it is wrong to excessively eat and drink, you create a healthy habit, replacing unhealthy food with healthy ones. In fact, you are creating an alternative to your old beliefs.

- Creating an alternative – the fifth step which strengthens change is the creation of an alternative. You can't just settle when you've eliminated one habit which pulled you down, but you need to create another one, which will propel you forward. If you've managed to quit smoking, it's time to make a plan for the future, otherwise, you will fall into other addictions that will lead to the same fate as before. Build an alternative that you keep rehearsing until it becomes a habit and then you are saved.

The secret of success lies in the appreciation and gratification of every step you make. For a real change, you have to celebrate every success, no matter how small it may be, because then you feel appreciated, fulfilled, happy and motivated to keep on going. How can you achieve this? There are many methods that can be used:

- By appreciation – meaning to use all sorts of positive and encouraging words, through which you assess your progress. Don't wait for others to appreciate you; do it yourself.
- By reward or gratification – don't just thank yourself for the progress made, with appreciation, but do more: acknowledge those appraisals, in order for the motivation to be even stronger. Repay yourself with a movie, a vacation, a night out in the city, with a romantic dinner

with your wife or friends... Think of the reward you can afford as a result of quitting an addiction and saving money. In addition, you might have some money left for savings.

If beside you people are ready to support you in the process of changing a habit or with the elimination of an addiction, then tell them what you want to do before you start, in order to receive the necessary motivation and have them by your side throughout the change process. When others appreciate our progress, we feel much more motivated to continue. However, if you don't have someone beside you, then seek to appreciate yourself. You can solely change anything. The secret is to keep yourself motivated and passionate during the change. Encouragement is the soul's oxygen.

- Creating a target – this step is about discovering the reason you want to change. What is it? You probably want to become responsible or disciplined. This is a good approach, but still, you haven't found the source of motivation. The target you set in front of you must be motivating. In order to do this, first, you need to discover what is the most important to you.

Ask yourself what is the thing that you treasure the most and in which you would be ready to invest anything, even if this implies suffering. That thing is different for each individual;+ some are passionate about their career, in which they restlessly work; others are passionate about their life partner, about their dream, about the business they wish to develop, about children, etc. For some people, God is above everything.

What is the thing you value most and for which you'd be willing to suffer? If you've discovered it, then set it in front of you, because it will be the target, but at the same time, the reason you will change any habit and any negative belief that pulls you down. When your brain understands the mechanism, it will work towards obtaining the end result, achieving the target. In this battle of transformation, you'll form an extremely powerful character. However, the only thing you can't change is the one that you're not motivated enough to do so. If motivation exists then you can accomplish the impossible.

- The reward – with each passing day, you must appreciate yourself for your accomplishments. If you overcame the temptation to resume to your old habit, then congratulate yourself in that exact moment in order for your brain to perceive the benefits. If, however, you fail and fall, begin again. In this situation, it is very important you focus on the profound pain, in order to imprint the negative effect in your mind.

Let's suppose that you no longer want to be late. You've proposed to yourself to become a punctual person, no matter what situation you encounter. When you managed to reach the target, celebrate this success. Feel accomplished and proud. But if you don't manage to do so, feel the pain of the failure. Feel deeply aggrieved, unfulfilled and ashamed about the delay. In this manner, the brain will understand and will find the necessary motivation to change this habit.

8

First Step

Where and how you'll end up are linked with your initiative. More specifically, where, when, and if you start. If now, you take action and apply everything you've learned to your life, then the way you'll end up will be a positive one. The same will be true for every emotion, circumstance, thought, belief, choice, action and result that you experience. People who take initiative and start to make changes, have all the chances to succeed, but those who don't take initiative are heading towards one destiny: failure.

I am sure that up until now, you've discovered things that you have to change, that slow you down or misguide you from the place you want to reach. I bet that there is a habit that you should change, a belief that you should replace, a principle that you should form, an addiction that you should give up, a character component that you should assimilate, or a value that you should prioritize. If you want to get somewhere and become the person you want to be, then now is the time to act.

You now know what you have to do in order to obtain the long-awaited change and maybe you know why you didn't think it imperative to do so before.

In any of these situations, you must be committed 100%. From this point on, you truly start living. The time of simply surviving is done, it's time for accomplishments.

We talked about so many things that lead to success once they are applied, but the change itself will continue to be just a dream, until the moment we take the first step. It is the one that will make a difference in all that we have learned so far, whether it's the habits you want to change, beliefs, or addictions we want to put behind us, financial statements, career or dreams.

Although the first step is the most important one, most do not take it. We study what we want to change, we learn many things, but we rarely act. No matter what you want to change in your life, the first step is the most important, because the next will come naturally, with a bit of perseverance. In order to take the first step, you must feel sufficiently motivated so as to be willing to go through short term pain, for a lifetime change.

Things you need to be motivated

1) Enthusiasm – Offers everything you need to get started. Is the one that leads to action? If you don't feel motivated enough, you'll never be ready to take the first step.

2) Passion – Provides continuity of the enthusiasm that led you to take that first step. The first step is just the beginning, that's why you want to keep on going. Have you ever been so excited in a certain moment, that you've felt you could turn the world upside down? I've felt it and I think you have too. These moments represent what you need to get started. These are the early days of the desire to change, but after a few days, gradually, you feel like that the enthusiasm is no longer the same. Now, you don't know if you can continue further, although before you were 100% sure. Over time, you become increasingly vulnerable and tempted to return to your old life.

The question that arises is: how to remain focused on change, without losing motivation? The answer is passion. To continue the process, even if the enthusiasm is not the same, you have to find that thing that keeps you passionate and eager. What is the thing for which you would be willing to suffer, to lose, to sacrifice, to work, if needed? For each of us, that thing is different. In some cases, it may even be themselves, though this is rare. For others, it could be the wife, girlfriend, partner or children; the dream and desire to achieve that dream; career, influence, popularity; desire to help others; faith in God; economic stability or happiness.

What is that thing for you? Seek to discover it because it is the key to success. Something will represent the source of passion which will nurture your enthusiasm to continue. Once found, put it in front of you, so as to repeatedly remind you why you want it. A passionate person is unstoppable.

In the change process that you initiated, repeat to yourself why you want to change something: "I want to change because only in this way I will fulfill my dream!" "I want to change to be loved by God!" "I want to change to be better for my family!" "I want to change in order to create a better financial situation!" Whatever the reason, keep it and repeat it, because it provides the needed passion.

3) Dedication – The next thing that needs to be done is to dedicate yourself to that change. Dedication means putting aside your time, to continuously find solutions which will lead towards the resolution and implementation of the proposed plan. It is possible that, somewhere along the way, you might fail the test and return to the habit you're trying to forget. Stand up and continue. Don't give up until you succeed!

4) Action – Dedication is real only when you act without interruption. If you do it just for a short period of time, the motivation will disappear. The action is what makes dedication authentic. Acting with passion and dedicating yourself to the plan of change will get the long-awaited results.

5) Environment – The environment around you will increase or decrease the chances of change. If you surround yourself with negative people, who only see the darkness, it will be twice as difficult to succeed. You can be the fastest person in the world, but if I put you in mud, you'll be slowed significantly. Surround yourself with positive people who encourage you in what you are doing and appreciate progress, however, small it may be. If you don't have this type of support group, you don't have to worry. You will manage alone, but then you have to be very careful to reject any negativity you encounter.

Furthermore, focus on the motivation and appreciation that you give yourself.

6) *Updating* – The last thing you need to do is update your approach continuously. Throughout this process, you will do things that will either propel you further or pull you back. There will be things that will help you significantly and things that won't. All these must be carefully analyzed and constantly updated.

Example: On a sheet of paper or wherever want you, write in two parallel columns, separated by a line, the following:

- Things that will help you significantly
- And things that slow the process down. Keep track of them in time, removing those that don't help and focusing only on those that bring improvement. In this way, you will avoid stagnation and obtain results.

A constant mistake which I see from people around me is they repeat a nonfunctional thing. It is impossible to have different results, as long as you make the same choices and repeat the same actions. For different results, you need to choose differently, that's why keeping track of the progress and updating data represents the secret towards success.

Thomas Edison is the person who understood the importance of keeping track of progress and of constant updates, in his attempt to create something that would burn without interruption, namely, the bulb. After a thousand failures, as those around him called it, he achieved the biggest success. Interviewed afterward he was asked what led him to persevere despite his repeated failures. Edison said, "I've never failed, not once. On the contrary, all this time I found method after method, which simply did not function." Edison considered what we call failure, another method that didn't work. He kept track of the things that worked and of those that didn't, accomplishing what he proposed. Every time he found a nonfunctional method, he wrote it down in order to avoid its repetition. In this way, every time he tried something new. Later on, after hundreds of discoveries that did not function, he finally found one that worked and changed the world forever.

The same is valid for me and you, if we want to really achieve what we propose. You must get rid of every method that doesn't function and focus on others, until, at some point, you discover the method that propels you forward, towards success.

The change process

By accepting the fact that you are now in a process of changing completely, I want to tell you how long it takes until a habit, an addiction or a belief is changed. Psychologists discovered that a person needs about thirty days for his mind and body to get used to a new routine. For reliable results, it must be practiced daily, in order to last even longer.

In the first ten days of the change process, you must get rid of the G-force- the gravitational force. The first ten days are crucial because your mind and body are in your comfort zone and will say "no, no, no". During these days it is mandatory to resist the signals your brain transmits and use your willpower to continue. The ten days of perseverance will make the difference and will lead to a new, positive and beneficial routine.

Between the 10th and 20th day of the change process, you will have to get rid of the R force- resistance. At this point, it is no longer as difficult as in the first days, however, there will be some resistance here and there. It is estimated that the signals from the old routine, the ones sent by the brain are in a small number and quite weak, being about two or three a day. These can be dismissed on the spot, so, by changing the focus, you will be able to continue without being affected by these signals.

Between the 20th and the 30th day comes the third process called A-acclimatization. Now you start getting used to the new routine. The brain renounces something and implements another thing. From this point on, you're safe, having a positive and beneficial routine. The wonderful part is that once formed, the new routine will go on its own. You no longer need the willpower to stop doing what you were doing before, nor to keep on doing what you do now because your brain will constantly signal you regarding what you have learned to practice.

Example: Let's suppose you've replaced an old habit with a new one. Before, you used to spend two hours watching TV or on social networking sites, but felt that this did not bring you any benefit and that you're wasting your time. Therefore, you set in mind to replace this old lifestyle of TV or the Internet with reading. For 30 days you have implemented the new habit, and at present, the investment in reading contributes to your personal growth and development.

Therefore, thirty days have passed since you made your first step and now you're enjoying the new beneficial habit. The beautiful part is that from now on, you no longer have to use your willpower to read, instead of watching television, because your brain has accepted the old habit as being negative and the new habit as being positive. In this manner, reading became something natural and is now is a part of you. In the past, the brain made you feel stupid if you didn't practice the old habit, but it now makes you feel stupid if you don't practice the new habit. This is the beautiful part, which results from the good habits. These can lead us either towards success or towards failure. You make choices taking into account the beliefs and habits that you assimilate daily.

It was argued that the ideas we create transform into reality. When you adopt positive thoughts about a thing, these become a belief on which you base choices in the future. Then, as a result of the belief, you will experience a positive result. In other words, what you visualize in your mind becomes reality.

Speaking and visualization

1) Inner dialogue through speech – is a form of subconscious programming, which requires you to be present at both ends of the dialogue. You speak to yourself. Typically, the dialogue consists of repeated sessions of questions and answers, stimulated by circumstances and the things around you. Inner dialogue tends to be an accidental dialogue, reactive rather than one thought. The question-answer format is the method by which the brain evaluates experiences. To benefit from this dialogue, we must communicate intentionally to the conscious mind what we want to do.

For example, if you want to change something, you have to communicate this change to the conscious mind. With the help of the list which I proposed earlier, with regard to things that you want to change, you will be able to clarify what you want to do and why. Then the brain will assimilate what you want and will become aware of the pluses and minuses, and will contribute to the desired change. Now, if you know what you want to change, write it on a sheet of paper and read it daily, until you notice that your belief has changed. Keep that worksheet and recite it loudly and clearly, until what you wrote is what you believe about yourself. Only then, will the change you want to experience be guaranteed.

An example of the power of the spoken word is Stephen Curry, an American professional basketball player in the National Basketball Association (NBA). He was declared the best performer in the history of basketball. In the year 2015, he won the award for the best player in the NBA. He led Golden States Warriors in the first league since 1975. In 2012, he set a record in the NBA with 272 points. In 2014 he has passed that record with 286 points. In 2015 he surpassed the record again with 382 points. He was named three times in a row, NBA all-star. All of these, are just a part of basketballer Stephen Curry's achievements.

You probably ask yourself, as I've asked myself, what is the reason behind this success? The secret lies in the conversation and visualization that we have with ourselves. Stephen has a motto in life, which he repeats every time he enters the field. It is Philippians 4:13: "I can do all things through Christ which enhances me". This verse landed him in the first place, and from there, he became the best in NBA history. In an interview, he said: "People should know who they are and who they represent: It's Jesus Christ! The reason I beat my chest and point upward, is because my heart beats for God."

The words that we tell ourselves can take us either to the top of success or limit us to the mediocrity in which most indulge. You alone are responsible for the words you tell yourself. If you say you can't or don't believe, then you won't achieve, but if you are full of positivism and passion, then nothing can stop you. Stephen Curry broke every record because he believed what he said, namely, that he can do anything through Christ, which strengthens him. Constantly saying these words means you'll end up believing what you say, and then you'll really be able to everything.

2) *Visualization* – Positive visualization is a technique of subconscious programming. It is accomplished by imagining the results before they take place in physical reality. Through visualization, a person can choose to imprint positive images in his mind, which will shape his thoughts and concentration. This technique is at everyone's disposal. Once you learn and acknowledge it, it will help you to create, change or improve any custom and belief, or to eliminate an addiction.

This practice called visualization is realized in the subconscious of all people, either positively or negatively. Most, however, are not aware of it; that's why they are driven by thoughts left to chance. Your subconscious is responsible for the success, failure, or your long-term mediocrity. If for instance, all kinds of negative thoughts exist, then you will be "forced" to visualize negative images. If you think positive thoughts, you will visualize positive images.

To fully benefit from this ability, we must learn to practice it by applying control over our thoughts. We either control them, or they will control us.

Positive and beneficial images will come as a result of the positive thoughts that we plant and which are related to the habit we want to create, with the belief or addiction we want to eliminate. For example, when we intentionally repeat out loud our beliefs that we acquired as a result of change, we adopt positive thoughts in our mind and create positive images. When we have positive images, the brain is informed of all the benefits that will result from the change, and all of all losses which we will suffer if we do not change, then we are motivated to replace that habit immediately.

For maximum results, you must:

• say loudly all the benefits and losses,
• imagine those benefits and losses in your mind.

Example: Let's suppose you want to change the bad habit of gossiping. In this situation, you have to go through important stages:

Negatively visualize: imagine in your mind how this habit transforms you into a distrustful person, but also into a friend that no one wants to have. Imagine that if you continue to gossip, everyone will avoid you, because they will be afraid that you'll to tell all their secrets. Imagine that God is unhappy with you because of your gossiping. Imagine that gossiping makes you a person without character and reflects your weakness.

All of these are negative images that you say out loud, which you visualize in your mind for an even greater impact. Understanding all of these, the brain will perceive how harmful this habit is for you and as a result, it will be open to change.

Positively visualize: Now, after you've visualized and become aware in your brain of all the negative parts, it is time to become aware of the gains that will result after the change occurs. Imagine the true friendship you will have and that others will be able to count on you. Imagine the trust that others will grant you. Imagine how God will see you now and how pleased He'll be. Imagine the self-esteem you will have.

All of these, and many other that you choose to positively visualize will help you get where you want and realize what you have proposed.

9

Thoughts

The human brain is the headquarters of thoughts and it's the most complex organ in the universe. Look around you and imagine that everything you see is the result of the brain, which operates through thoughts. Everything that mankind did, good or bad, began with a thought. Everything you currently accomplish or you have achieved so far is based on a thought. At one point, it was just a thought that, put into action, turned into a phone, house, and many other things. The source of millions of objects "came" from the same place called the brain, through the shape of the same thought. All our achievements have come as a result of thinking.

Thoughts are the source of prosperity, success, happiness, dreams, plans, and all discoveries, inventions, and achievements. Imagine that all the choices you make, good or less good, come from thoughts. Everything that you are is due to thoughts. Want to know why you acted in a certain way at a certain moment? The answer is: because of your thoughts. The beliefs and emotions that you feel in different moments have the same source called thought. Habits, addictions, curiosities have the same origin. Thoughts represent the spring of all the things in your life. Beliefs, habits, choices, actions and experiences, all are due to a person's thoughts. Thoughts represent the root of all things. What you see on the surface are the character, habits, and actions, but the real source lies inside, hidden in the mind. The mind is what produces everything we experience on the inside and out, through the thoughts we create.

"Seed a thought and you will reap an action, seed an action and you will reap a habit, seed a habit and you will reap a character, seed a character and you reap a destiny."
(Stephen Covey)

A person's beliefs are formed as a result of thoughts, and for the brain, thoughts are those images that help create the training process. Every thought that you experience is an image, which, together with another thought, can form a belief. Belief consists of many repeated thoughts gathered together. When the brain gathers enough information, thoughts, or images about a particular thing, it turns them into a belief.

For example, let's suppose that I offer you a cigarette for you to smoke. If you have a negative belief about smoking, you will definitely reject my proposal, and if I asked you why you'd come up with some negative arguments about smoking. Perhaps you'd tell me that it's not healthy, that it smells horrible, it is wasted money, causes cancer and produces stress and addiction. Of course, the list can go on depending on the person, but what I want you to notice is that each belief requires several pieces of information that represent the arguments for whether you believe or not, one way or another.

Belief starts at the level of thoughts. Once more thoughts about a particular thing are placed together, they form a belief. The important part is that for any new thing that you hear or experience, the brain forms a belief based on the image or definition you gave to the gathered information. To put it simply, in the future, if you want to create good beliefs, you need to be very careful about the thoughts that you receive in your heart and mind because they will define your trajectory in life. Each belief that you create in the future will help your growth if you understand how thoughts work.

The importance of thoughts

Thoughts are the most important battles that we have to face. Any victory or any failure firstly takes place in the mind. The devil will always struggle to control our thoughts because then he will win control over our lives. Thoughts are what produce beliefs, beliefs produce choices, and choices produce experiences.

Solomon said: "As a man thinks in his heart, so it is". If you truly want to direct your life in the desired direction, then you should start by controlling your thoughts. Be selective and don't let negative thoughts make room in your heart. Reject them! However, if it happens and you fall prey to these thoughts, don't persist in them. Even though we are sometimes not selective enough to stop them from entering our heads, we have the potential to replace them.

For example, if you have negative thoughts in a certain situation, without seeing a way out, it's a sign that you need to renounce those thoughts. Change them when you realize them. Do something different for ten minutes and disconnect. It's true, it takes time to renounce them forever and this varies from person to person. Try this and then look again at the situation you are facing and see what thoughts come to mind this time.

Attention! Negative thoughts will come over and over again, but now you're already paying attention to what you let in, and you've become selective. Look at all the choices that the brain presents to you and adopt the best positive choice. Only then will you be able to have clear thinking and relieve the pressure, taking the best decisions. Take control of your thoughts and you will be able to control your life. Thoughts are what give you information about the reality of life. If you have control over them, you will have control over your life, but if you don't have control over them, then they will rule your life. You will always be what you believe in your mind about yourself. In other words, you'll be like the thoughts you accept.

Psychologists state than the average person experiences between 20,000- 60,000 thoughts daily. Altogether these form the day, week, month, year, life and they define experiences, choices, and actions. Happiness, success, and fulfillment depend to a great extent on thoughts. Their importance is bigger than you've ever imagined. In fact, you are what you are because of the thoughts that you've accepted.

The best comparison regarding thoughts was used by Jesus. He said they are like birds flying above the house. None of us have the possibility to prevent them from flying over our homes, but each of us has the power to stop them from making a nest. Don't accept negative thoughts that make nests in your mind. I do not accept the idea of negative thoughts making nests in my brain.

Each of us has the possibility and power to decide if they let other's words affect them or not. As with personal thoughts. You and I are masters of our own minds. If you want to be sure of success in life, make sure you follow what Jesus said. The Holy Spirit whom God sent after Jesus's rising is the one who puts every positive and moral thought inside your mind, so, be sure that you become sensitive to His voice. Jesus is the author of an extraordinary life. A lifetime of success means a life in which Jesus is Lord over your mind, from which will result, all the positive thoughts that will shape your life.

Thoughts are those inner images that produce emotions and moods. To feel positive and energetic, all you have to do is think positively and be optimistic. Many people are passionate about certain things, at certain times, but after a while, they discover that the passion no longer exists. The reason is that those powerful thoughts, which were processed by the brain, such as: "I'll make a difference!", "I'll succeed!", "I'll change the world with God's help!" have turned into less positive thoughts like: "I don't know if I'll manage!", "It's too hard!", "I don't think I'm the right person, so God will choose another!" etc. This is the difference between the passionate and passive person. Thoughts lead to passion or to passivity and simultaneously generate the energy and enthusiasm needed to accomplish something.

What I want to emphasize is that the secret of a more enthusiastic, energetic, happy, accomplished life comes as a result of the thoughts you cultivate in your mind. A man is happy when he focuses his mind on beautiful and positive things. Another is unhappy because he focuses on the things he doesn't possess, on how weak he is or how unfair life is and so on.

God gave us our minds, which is part of our soul, to use it towards His glory and our fulfillment. But the devil fights for our soul, and hence, for our minds, and once he wins our soul, he possesses our life.

If there is something that must be protected more than anything on this Earth, it is the soul. Make sure that God is master over your soul and then your life won't have limitations, neither spiritual nor material. God is the author of a wonderful life and together with Him, life brightens up.

The source of thoughts

Every day, thousands of thoughts come into our mind, either positive or negative. However, what kind of thoughts you allow to remain in your brain depends on your choice and mine. Thoughts upon which we meditate and focus on will be stored in our brain, so we have to be selective with regards to them.

In the world, there are two forces: a good and a bad one, a positive and a negative one. All that you see around you is the result of the positive force, and what is bad is the negative force's doing. All the same, there are only two kinds of people: people who think positively and people who think negatively. Everyone fits into one of these two ways of thinking. What you choose to think will determine what you experience. If you choose to think negatively (that you won't succeed, you're not talented enough, you don't have what it takes), then surely, the action will be as you believe, leading to limitation. If, however, you choose to believe that you can, you have everything you need and that you will succeed, then nothing will be able to stop you from succeeding.

If you are a pessimistic person and you find it difficult to change something, then allow me to give you good news. Nobody was born with a pessimistic or an optimistic attitude. Every individual's thinking was formed during his life. Society, family, friends and everyone else with whom you come into contact transformed you into what you are. Negativity is like the flu, it's contagious, but the same is true of positivity. If you're a negative person, all you need to do is to read books that help you develop and surround yourself with positive people, who possess the gift of faith.

The devil will try to negatively influence you through every negative person around you, so you continue to be limited. The smaller and insignificant you are, the better for him, because you won't be a problem. God gave you everything you need to make a difference, but the devil will try to lie to you and provide all sorts of excuses to prevent your success. He will fight so he can coordinate, urge and guide you as he pleases. However, both, you and I have control, not of what others do, but of what we are doing.

God is the author and creator of any person and any nice and positive thing. He created us with a positive human nature, to be good, but because of the existence of sin, the devil has access to our mind and he can influence us negatively. Attention! The only thing that the devil can do is to seed a negative thought of fear, worry, concern, immorality, in order to determine us to act against God's will. However, you must be aware that the final decision belongs to you. You and I decide if we are going to let that thought into our brains, as Jesus said, or if we reject it. He does not have control over you if you don't let him. However, he can seed a tempting and clever thought through which you'll take action.

No person in the universe is bad, on the contrary. God created all of us to be very good, but every person may, to a greater or less extent, do good or bad, depending on the thoughts he accepts. If for example, you see someone that does harm, you can imagine that the devil controls his thoughts, through which he influences the person's beliefs, then their choices and actions.

People do harm in the wake of the negative thoughts that they have accepted in their minds. Some are very moral, sincere, trustworthy and benevolent, but sometimes they do a nasty thing, which causes amazement to those who know them. In those moments, they experience exactly what I was saying, meaning they lose control over their thoughts and are lured by the devil to do that ugly thing. Any "space" created in the mind for negativism will lead to negative actions and choices, which will bring about negative experiences. These are moments of confusion, exploited by the devil through our thoughts.

At the same time, you will see people who do much harm, but sometimes, do good deeds as well. Unconsciously, these people granted the control to the devil and he operated through them and brought his dirty and corrupt plans to an end. However, these people can also do good things, if they let the good act through them. The bottom line is that our actions are the result of the forces which control us; that's why you don't have to follow anyone. And if we see some that do unlawful things, let's not forget that, unfortunately, they are captives of evil, who need help. This is the reason we should love all humans. By loving them, we will judge less, forgiving them more quickly and we will be able to help them. They are God's creation, but, unfortunately, the devil has control over them. If we approach them properly, we can change their beliefs and release them, to think freely and change their lives.

Just think of one thing that you detest and then find the explanation for this. Whatever the reason, it is actually the image you've created about that thing. What I want you to understand is that you form an image (positive or negative) about a certain thing, and later, the brain reminds you what you've convinced it to believe about that thing. If you look carefully inside, you will notice that every piece of information has an assigned image. In other words, each new person we meet and any new thing that we experience is checked by our brain. If it doesn't find any information, it continues to process until it obtains a positive or negative image, which it stores in memory. Pay attention to what you allow to "sit" in your mind as that will later influence your life.

Everything we experience along the way adds up to thoughts because that's the starting point for everything. Every belief is formed as a result of your thoughts. Each choice is based on what you think. Every action is due to thoughts. In other words, everything you experience in life is due to the thoughts you allow in your mind and which make a nest there.

Allow me to ask what kind of thoughts you let in your mind, positive or negative ones? Do you have control over the thoughts that pass daily through your mind? Your answer will determine each experience, that's why I want to help you create a filter for your thoughts. With this help, you will become more selective, wiser in every choice you make in the future.

Checking thoughts

In order to have positive beliefs, we must ensure that we have total control over the thoughts that settle in our minds. Every thought is an image of one of the two forces which will influence both our emotional status and beliefs or choices. How can I redirect your life positively, so you are in a state of permanent growth? By controlling and carefully checking the thoughts which settle in the mind. You should never allow thoughts of fear, worry, helplessness, weakness, immorality to make room in your brain. They will influence you to act less wisely. To discover and verify the nature and effects of your thoughts, I advise you to use the filter method. Then, it's up to you to make the right choice.

1) Filter

- What do my thoughts produce, negativity or positivity? Through this question, you will be able to observe the nature of the thoughts which try to settle down in your mind. If these produce fear, distrust, concern, discouragement, then they are sent from the devil and should be rejected immediately.
- Do these thoughts break God's morality? Through this question, you will be able to observe if they lead to morality or immorality, to growth or downfall. If, for example, those thoughts are incompatible with God's values, then, it will have a negative effect in your life. Thoughts of stealing, lying, gossiping, greed, violence, abuse... and the list goes on, are from the devil; that's why we must reject them, otherwise, they will lead you on a negative path.
- What will those specific thoughts produce in my life if I accept them: growth or downfall? Ask yourself what kind of effect they will have on your life, if you accept them in your heart. Will it create good or bad beliefs? Will it bring benefit or not? Will it make you a better person, or a bad one? Will it strengthen your character or will it affect it? Will it help you choose well or not?

These questions will help you discover the nature of your thoughts that pass daily through your mind. If these are positive and beneficial, these must be received and developed, but if they are not beneficial, they must be rejected.

2) Choice

- Identification - the first thing that you will conclude from checking your thoughts is the nature of their provenience.
- Provenance - by asking yourself questions from your filter, you will notice if the thoughts are positive or negative if they are from God or from the devil. After you've checked and found from whom they come, you'll move forward to the next step.
- Acceptance or rejection- we now know where the thoughts come from, therefore, based on their origin, we will decide what we will do with them. If they have a positive nature, then we put them into practice and act upon them. Choosing in this manner, we will experience the positivity. If they have a negative nature, then they should be rejected immediately and we should change the focus, otherwise, it will negatively affect us and we don't want this.

Thoughts' effects

Positive thoughts have the power to attract prosperity, health, happiness, and fulfillment, while negative thoughts have the power to keep you away from all the wonderful things that God prepared for you. Positive thoughts propel you to the peak of the mountain, while negative thoughts pull you downwards to the valley. Every thought that you accept into your mind and concentrate upon, influences you directly, positively or negatively, becoming presumed truths. Without a filter, thoughts enter your mind and form beliefs which affect your every choice.

If the thoughts you've accepted are positive, they will create positive beliefs which become monuments to success and will allow you to continuously persevere, think, and work for your dreams until they become reality. The more positive a person is, the more he will become happier, stronger and more creative. The good news is that you can also become a positive person. All you have to do is make sure that you filter the thoughts perceived by your mind.

People who accept negativity are also the people who create excuses for anything they are told. Excuses come in all possible forms, but their effects are highly damaging, just like a disease that weakens you daily until you manage only to survive instead of truly living. The following three excuses are the most commonly encountered:

1) Intelligence – "I am not smart enough, I'm not qualified enough, I'm not valuable enough, I am not talented enough..." You must realize that the most important people in history, who changed the world, were simple people with great thoughts. Howard Schultz, the man who was originally manager of the marketing department and supply chain of Starbucks, who later bought the company, turning it into the world's market leader, grew up in a poor family. His success is due to his positive attitude. Albert Einstein, considered mentally retarded and antisocial in his childhood, become a genius with the highest IQ, not because he let himself influenced by negativity, but because he decided to release the intelligence that God gave him.

Now, while reading this book, I want to ask yourself something. Stop reading, take a minute and think of all your achievements, diplomas, all things that you own, and everything you are. Visualize this and see if all of these are only a percentage of what you could become if you'd think differently about yourself.

2) Age – "I'm too old" or "I'm too young" become the best excuses for most people. These people know exactly what pretexts to invent for not doing more, for not achieving or fighting more. "I am too old", they say, now it's your turn to do something. "It doesn't matter how old you are; if you think positively, nothing will be able to stop you from achieving what God has put in your heart."

McDonald's is the world's largest fast-food chain, which serves over 68 million people daily in over 119 countries. It was founded by Richard and Maurice McDonald after they passed the age of 50 years old. Kentucky Fried Chicken is another fast-food chain founded by Colonel Sanders at the age of sixty years, after a thousand failed attempts. Ronald Reagan became President of the United States just a few days before turning seventy years old.

Age is not an obstacle for those who have a positive mindset, but on the contrary, it is one more reason to prevail. Age can mean either the ticket towards success, which brings all of life's experience, training, and maturity or the reason you're called "too old", which will prevent your success. You decide which you pick.

"I am too young" is another myth that stops many people from becoming and realizing what lies in their power. Bill Gates, the richest man in the world, established the Microsoft Company when he was just twenty years old. Steve Jobs created Apple Company when he wasn't even twenty years old. You're never too young, you're never too old to follow your dream. Change your thinking and you'll change your life.

The attitude we adopt is the one that makes a difference, not age.

3) Health – This excuse is invoked by the same large number of people, who complain about all health issues they have. Accept the fact that nobody is perfectly healthy and that everyone has reasons to complain about their health, although not everyone accepts them as excuses for failure. What category do you belong to?

Excuses regarding health do nothing but alienate others from being around you, because nobody wants to deal with negative people, who complain about every pain they have, no matter how small it is. And if there are some who sit and listen to all your complaints, it's because they're alike. Nobody loves pain, therefore, when talking about it, people tend to become estranged from you, because you make room for pain in their lives.

Studies show that the negative words you articulate in this moment, such as "my head hurts", end up causing exactly the state of mind that you're complaining about. All you have to do is think that you have a headache and repeatedly say it and the brain will produce it. The good news is that things work the same way in reverse, or when you say: "I'm healthy, agile and nothing hurts". If you come out as the winner from the battle with your thoughts, you will also win the physical and mental battle.

Next time you feel tempted to use an excuse instead of taking action, just think of all the people who struggled with pain and defeated it, becoming successful. If you want to be great, you have to think big. Decide to set aside any excuses and use your intelligence, creativity, potential, and the opportunities that God gives you on a daily basis.

Positive or negative, all actions have a single source, the thoughts. Control them and you'll control your life.

Neural associations

Associations you create in your mind lead to choices and subsequently, to actions. You always have to be careful about the type of associations you make. Through the respective associations, you create a definition that you'll experience when you have decided and concluded the association. If you put a bad label on a good thing, you will experience it as such. For example, if you associate love with grief, then you'll avoid love, which is actually the key ingredient to preventing pain. Many people with whom I speak associate pain with love, and as a result, they avoid love.

People who suffered enormously in a relationship, fixed in their mind, the idea that love is the source of the pain, so now they live with a fear of love. If you've loved a person greatly and she cheated on you or disappointed your expectations, then you will unintentionally assign love as the cause of your pain. At the same time, you will connect your relationship and partner with the cause of the pain, and because this association is wrong, you will wake up believing that you're afraid to love or to enter into a relationship with a partner, without knowing why.

The brain gathers information constantly and makes connections with others until it reaches a conclusion. It is very important to understand that information results from our concentration.

For example, if you focus on inequity or on the pain that you have suffered, you'll almost certainly reach a negative conclusion. But if you focus on the positive side of your experience, you will reach a positive conclusion. Each association will lead to a specific emotional state. If you associate the difficulty you've gone through with negativity or injustice, you will have feelings related to this, but if you associate it with shaping and growth, you'll have a positive state of mind, because you see the good side of that specific situation.

Allow me to ask you your perception of this issue? How do you relate to people around you when they do wrong? To clarify this, watch the way you experience it. Why can a person remain positive even in the midst of a problem, of pain, or on a rainy day? Because he chooses to see the full cup. A rainy day has its benefits, which are just as important as those of a sunny day. On a rainy day, look out for the rainbow, on a sunny day, look out for the sun.

Every day is a reason to please God if you take it as a blessed day. In each moment of your life, you have a choice to make, namely: what thoughts do you allow into your mind? Each association is determined by thoughts that transform into images, and if repeated, become beliefs. If you want to be in control of the situation, regardless of the circumstances, make sure you're in control of your thoughts. Use the filter to recognize their origin and thus, your life will be different from now on.

Two things contribute to how we perceive the reality around us and they are:

1) *The emotional state*

It is possible to build a belief based on your emotional well-being, and that will influence your future, starting from choices, up to consequences.

Have you ever gone to a certain place and disliked everything, despite the beautiful things that you found there? Have you ever wondered why? Then, do you remember how good you felt the second time you went there, in a positive mood? How is it possible you missed this the first time? Because you interpreted everything based on your mood, and state you were in, blocking the beautiful moments and experiences.

Do you remember those moments when someone you loved had a problem? You tried everything in your power to change the situation and did all sorts of things that once, the person in question, would have appreciated enormously, but nothing worked? Well, his emotional state contributed to this. Now, if an emotional state is just an indisposition, it will pass. However, what is extremely important is that you never form a belief when you're in that state of mind. Why? Because it will continue to affect you every time you look at that person, place or thing in question.

I've lost count of the people with such beliefs, whom I've met over the years. These people formed a belief while they were in a state of ailment. Since that moment, even if their state of mind has changed, the way in which they respond to that belief remains the same. Particularly important in the formation process is the image through which you interpret and define a particular belief. If you look at your life, you can easily discover things or places that you dislike. You believe it is normal to be this way, huh? Although I believe there are things, places, or people that don't attract us as much as others do, the difference is made by the way we associate them with our state of mind.

Let's suppose that you love a certain place so much, that only thinking about it makes you feel positive. It's your favorite place! Have you ever wondered why you like it so much? The answer is simple: because you've positively interpreted it. Once your brain associated positively with that specific place, you gave it a positive image and from that moment on, it became a positive belief, which influenced your feelings and state of mind. Because you had the appropriate state of mind and the association was positive, that place turned into something pleasant for you.

Have you ever wondered why two people who are in the same place give a totally different definition of that location? This is due to the connection they've created in their mind. Through the thoughts that they've put together, they define what that place means to them.

At one point, a friend of mine and I went through that same experience. We both went to Norway to work for a higher salary. After arriving there, I was fascinated by all the beautiful things that I had encountered. I was impressed by everything I saw and experienced, and the image I formed in mind was increasingly positive. Not long after, that place became my second home. I was happy and fully satisfied with the people there, with the place, friends, salary, serenity, but less with the rain. The only thing I disliked was the rain because I wasn't used to so much, but other than that, everything was beautiful.

In contrast, my friend experienced the exact opposite. From the beginning, he found everything beautiful as well. But it didn't last long. Within just two weeks, the beautiful image would turn into a negative belief. After two years, for my friend, coming to Norway was an ordeal. Everything seems to be negative when seeing it through his eyes. However, he was compelled to stay, because he was a seasonal worker for about half a year. Every time I met him, he would say how horrible he felt and describe how he couldn't wait to return home. He even reached the point of counting the remaining days, which meant a physical and psychological torment. He was always tired and bored, and the answer to my question regarding the reason was the same: the place. For a period of time I did not understand why he hated Norway so much, but later I realized that the reason was simple: the negative belief that he formed.

The way you characterize a place in your mind, through the thoughts you transform into images, matters. A certain place could turn into paradise or hell, depending on how you associate it in your mind. You decide! If you are one of those people who can't adapt in the place they are, then you should ask yourself what belief you have formed about that place, because it is a negative one.

For two years, my friend experienced an ordeal during his stay in Norway, until I helped him understand that he had the power to decide what that place meant to him. The reason he began disliking Norway is that he formed a negative image of it. During the first two weeks, he was really impressed, visiting and exploring one place after another. But, after exhausting all the important touristic points in the area in which he was working, he asked himself: "is that all?" From here started all his disappointment and since that moment, he saw only the negative things, such as rain, cool weather, low rate of population, and focused on them. These things changed his opinion, and from that moment on, his stay in Norway meant a constant state of negativity.

On the other hand, I realized that a low number of people means more peace and less stress. So, what created frustration for my friend, became a blessing for me. If for him that place meant a torment, to me it was my second home.

You've probably found yourself in such a situation, or gone through such moments when a specific place has negative connotations. Perception and pairings in your mind will affect your stay there, and if it happens to be like my friend's situation, where you are forced to stay in a place because of work, you will have a lot to lose. The good news is that regardless of the belief you have formed consciously or not, it can be changed, if you choose to change it. The place you hate now can become your second home, or your dream location. After I told my friend the reason for his struggling and negative moods, my friend understood and accepted he could change his impression, using the model I gave him. After just a few weeks, he went from being the frustrated, sad, and dull person he was, to a positive, excited and energetic person.

The way you interpret an image about a place or a particular thing makes the difference. Happiness in life is not necessarily given by the place you're in, but by how you perceive it. Between two people who find themselves in the same place, one is enjoying every moment spent, and the other hates every second. You need to understand that everything that you experience comes in the wake of the choice made in your mind about that particular place. Belief comes from the thoughts you focus upon.

For every negative or positive, pleasant or unpleasant thing that you perceive, you've formed a belief. The brain is the master in accumulating information, so every new thing is turned into an image, based on the experiences we go through. If it happens that a new thing that you experience for the first time produces a negative state of mind or affects you in any way (physical, mental or spiritual), the brain automatically transforms it into a negative image, which aims to protect you in the future. The brain was designed by God to protect us from anything negative, therefore, its role is to help us get as much pleasure, happiness, and positivity as we can and stop everything that means negativity or pain. Every fear that we have comes from certain experiences and from the way they were perceived by the brain.

My wife is a fine example of what it means to involuntarily form a negative image about something positive. Being in high school during a winter, she experienced a situation that she interpreted negatively. During school breaks, her colleagues took several girls by force, including her, and shoved them in the snow. My wife's health was affected, and she experienced a fever and lung infection the second day. She stayed in the hospital for more than three months in order to recover completely. What you need to know about her is that she loves winter sports, especially skiing, but not snow. Although it sounds strange, it's true. Of course, in order to practice skiing, you need snow, but for her, snow meant anxiety, stress, and concern.

When I realized this and saw how real the feeling was, I wanted to know the reason for it. Her response was that this is what she feels and that she doesn't like snow. That was it. However, she had no problem with winter. Understanding that there was something wrong with the concept in question, I asked her about the experience she went through regarding snow. Then she remembered that moment in high school. The next question was if she hated the snow in childhood and the answer was absolutely not. The reality is that when she experienced that complication because of snow, her brain chose to remember three things:

- How the event happened (in the snow);
- The season in which the event occurred (in winter);
- The element that contributed to that event (snow).

As a rule, the brain checks where, how, and when the relevant event occurred, and then comes up with a definition for the cause of the pain, ensuring that its repetition is avoided in the future. In my wife's case, the cause was the snow which made her cold and ill. Since that moment, a fear formed in her brain, which brought with it anxiety or displeasure whenever she saw snow. When I understood this, I helped her change her belief, and over time, that feeling has faded.

Many people experience such situations without having a clear cause. Many find themselves with certain fears, which they cannot explain. Some attempt to establish relationships but fail every time. The reason is the same: the fear of possible new suffering, although in most cases the previous problem was not the relationship itself, but the partner. If we are not careful, the brain wrongly interprets things and we find ourselves distrusting people.

The same is true in a business. Many of those who failed, instead of investigating the cause, give in to pressure, and in their minds, they establish that the business is the source of the problem. For this reason, they close up to the idea of a new business in the future. Others invest large sums of money in certain things, and they link the cause of the loss with the investment, and not with the things invested in or the specific circumstances. Now, for them, a new investment represents the biggest fear; that's why they sabotage themselves.

No matter the field in which we experience fear, it determines the renunciation of our dreams. The reason for abandoning or thinking of doing this thing is the impression formed in the mind, as a result of negative experiences. Make sure that you are the one who decides what kind of thoughts you receive or reject, and use the filter, in order to ensure a productive, beneficial, and successful functionality of the mind.Knowing these things, you will understand what the secret of a three-dimensional life is. For a successful life, it is vital to understand how the brain works, in order to protect it from anything that comes from the devil. The beautiful life that we imagine is nothing else but the result of the soul or mind directed correctly.

2) Expectations

Expectations are those prejudices or imaginary products of the mind that a person forms with respect to another person, place, or thing. Is that something that you expect to find when you stand face to face with reality? Expectations are normal and good, but only when they are correct.

Have you ever formed an idea about a person, depending on the information received from a friend or through a website, an image, etc.? Surely, we've all experienced this. What happened was the result of information received, which created an image of a certain person, and based on that image, you have created a particular expectation. Following the meeting with that person, you discovered that your expectations were either not met or were exceeded.

The same can happen with the place that you've decided to visit. You searched for information, saw pictures, and formed some expectations. You went there, but the situation proved to be different than what you imagined, so you got disappointed and fell into a state of ailment. No matter how hard you tried to find something positive, you didn't succeed.

We must be very careful in such moments because they can influence our beliefs and choices. It is important to understand that what we say about a person to another one, can later affect other people's expectations. Isn't it true that someone told you about another person, about how bad, horrible, arrogant, distrustful a person is, but after meeting with him, you saw that the reality was altogether different? How many times have you been surprised to discover an entirely different person than the one that was described to you? It happens frequently to me. However, I am very careful about the information I let contribute to the forming of an image because I do not want to create a wrong belief. Be very careful about what you hear about other people. Never judge nor gossip based on received information. Be selective! We must love everyone. Jesus loved us all up to the end, whatever our mistakes. As such, we are called upon to do the same.

Focusing contributes to the way you feel in each moment and to the way you interpret a place, a person, or a thing. Any of these can be viewed in one of two ways: positive or negative. You can go to the most beautiful place on Earth, but don't you feel good there. The place doesn't make the difference, but the things you want to see.

Focus on the positive things and you will feel positive, focus on the negative things and you will feel negative. What you seek to see in a person makes all the difference. If you focus on beautiful things, nice gestures, courtesy, well-defined character, humor then you'll feel good in the person's presence, but if you focus on the negative ones, you'll definitely feel negative. No matter who we are or what we are, we all have both good qualities and flaws.

To some, the balance is weighted to the good qualities, while for others, it is weighted to the flaws. However, no one is completely bad, as, no one is completely good. Each of us must decide what to focus on when talking about people who cross our path. Focus on qualities and you'll form a good belief, that will bring beautiful experiences; focus on the flaws and negatives and then your belief will be negative, and so will the experiences.

Never create a belief while being influenced by an extreme emotional state, whether it is positive or negative. Such a state of mind manipulates the way you relate to that thing. You can be in a very good mood and still be mistaken in your interpretation, therefore, pay attention to this thing. Is it normal to pass through such emotional states as a result of the surrounding events, but let's not forget that in these moments, you can choose how you will respond.

The success of an individual results from his thinking. The one who cultivates positive thoughts like: "I have potential, I am smart, capable, I'll make a difference in the world, I will succeed in what I have proposed, I will become a successful person", etc. will reap positive experiences. The one who cultivates negative thoughts such as "I don't have what I need, I am not capable, I will never succeed, others are smarter, with larger facilities than I have." will reap negative experiences. What you sow, that you will reap. Man's number one enemy is self-loathing, which occurs at the level of the mind. The devil puts all sorts of negative thoughts there, to keep him away from the accomplishments that might otherwise have.

The mind is like a garden whose gardener is you. Each individual cultivates what he wants. No one has the power to decide what to cultivate in your garden, except you. Those around us can bring their influence, but the choice belongs to us. If we focus on positive thoughts, we'll obtain positive beliefs that will lead to positive experiences; if we focus on negative thoughts, we get negative beliefs that will lead to negative experiences. An arranged, cared for, and daily nurtured garden produces fruit, vegetables, flowers, and it wonderful. When it is well taken care of, weeded and arranged, it will produce quality products, but when it is not, all that will occur will be thorns, weeds, and savage wildlife. There is also a third possibility, namely to produce fruit, vegetables, and flowers of poor quality, according to the care received.

Our brain is that garden that produces actions and experiences. But, what we must acknowledge is that these will always come as a result of the care given to the mind. If you do not watch your thoughts, beliefs, and choices deliberately, the results will be very weak or even harmful. Be an extraordinary gardener for your garden, called the brain, banishes all that attacks and stops your growth as a person, and you will see that your life will change radically.

10

Character

The character is the sum of a person's thoughts, beliefs, and actions, or, in other words, exterior behavior. Choices are indicators that describe the character, and actions show who we truly are. A person's character is the interior mirror which reflects what he is, starting from the simplest choices and continuing with his words and deeds. Lack of character limits us. A limited and mediocre person is always the result of a mediocre character. A man's character is the result of habits and beliefs taken together. In other words, if by this time, you have changed your negative habits and beliefs, you will have formed a positive, optimistic character. A strong character will always be above others. You will be more appreciated, smarter, capable, agile, controlled. You will motivate others to follow.

In a survey conducted on 385 millionaires, made over a period of five years, it has been discovered that success is determined by character. These people were responsible, had a positive attitude, they were tenacious, patient in achieving success, brave and incorruptible.

The word "character" originates from the Greek language, where it means chipper. In other words, character is that work of art resulted by manufacture, just like a statue is the result of chipping granite or marble. On a daily basis, each of us must eliminate all the useless sides, through our own work, until we become a work of art. Character proves what you are and what you have. Nobody can show more than he is. The biggest wish that we must have in life is the formation of a strong, well-defined character, otherwise, we sabotage ourselves through the choices we make, through the habits we have and beliefs that push us to take decisions. Most people fail to see their beautiful dream become reality because they didn't understand that their dreams are the result of a strong character. If you do not take the decision that leads you towards transformation, your character will not undergo any change for the better.

No one is born with a default character. It does not form automatically, but it must be transformed intentionally. It is, therefore, important how we respond to each circumstance (favorable or malevolent). No matter if you win or lose, what you decide to do next depends on you. Growth, maturation, learning, does not depend on luck, misfortune, chance, or injustice, but on how we adjust ourselves to every experience.

We all know people who make the same mistakes numerous times and still, they haven't learned anything from them; it can be said that they didn't use the opportunities to change something in their life so that their character remained ineffective. The most important condition is to want to learn all you can from each experience, mistake, success etc. So, choose to learn and form your character, regardless of the situations you find yourself in. You're the sculptor of your own character and God helps you only if you want and accept help. Choose to transform your character into an extremely valuable piece of art.

Eight components that define character

1) Integrity

When we have integrity in our lives, the words we utter correspond to our choices and our actions. The credibility of a person can be reduced to the word integrity, which defines our character. Incorruptible people are like an open book. They have nothing to hide, on the contrary, what they are in public they are also in their private life. Integrity means to say what you are doing and do as such. Who we are inside is shown through our actions.

Integrity is defined as the number of beliefs that we've gathered in our inner man. If the beliefs are upright, then the choices will be the same. An incorruptible person chooses on the basis of values and principles, not according to what he feels he should choose. He thinks, chooses and does. In addition, integrity predestines what and how we'll do, even before experiencing a thing. The trust that people grant us is defined by the integrity that we show. In order for me and you to be appreciated and respected, we need integrity. Success in life is defined by one's integrity. Whether we are talking about a position, career, potential, influence or relationship, all have integrity as a base.

The image from which people define you results from your integrity. Without integrity, it's only a matter of time until the trust you are granted is broken and the truth is exposed. A person lacking integrity doesn't lose only the trust of those around them, but also the influence he has upon them. People's motivation to stay near you depends on the confidence they can have in you.

Lying is the number one enemy of integrity which destroys the future of the one who practices it. A lie in a relationship will destroy it. A lie in a business will lead to bankruptcy. A lie in a society will destroy it. A lie has short legs. A lie will always lead to another one so that a rupture in the character becomes a crack. From then on, it's just a matter of time until the trust of those around will disappear. Be an honest person who says what he does and does what he says. Then you will direct yourself on the path towards success.

A man with character will always succeed in the long term, but the one without character may succeed in the moment but in time, will end up worse off. Check your values and beliefs about integrity and see in which areas of your life you say something other than what you do or do something other than what you say. Change what you need to and start going on the right and correct path. If for example, you cannot keep your word, then you have to check what certainties you have inside about honesty and sincerity. Ask yourself how do you feed your integrity, or on the contrary, your lies. Are you afraid of any chance? Do you think you cannot withdraw because you already lied and you must keep on going? It is because the lie gives you the feeling of winning? Do you believe that if you lie, you will manage to succeed in some way?

I have identified three kinds of people who lie:

- People who lie because of their beliefs. These are the ones who have lied to themselves with a lie that they promoted, believing that this will bring gain. They believe that in this way they will gain more, or that they'll get away with it, when in fact, the exact opposite will happen. On the spot, the lie may produce gains because it helps them get out of a mess. Over time, however, it will prove that they have entered into an even bigger lie. This is true in business, in relationships, in leadership. Now, you might sell your product based on deceit, but prepare yourself for the situation when you reach the top and fall directly on your head. Whatever you choose, integrity is a virtue that you cannot dispense of.
- People who lie due to habits. These people are already convinced that lying makes them important, so for them, lying means breathing. They cannot cope without lying because they have practiced this for a long period of time. More specifically, I can say that they are dependent on lying. If you are part of this category, of those who say something and do another, then, by all means, you should get rid of this habit. Identify the cause of lying and immediately change this habit, using the given pattern.
- People who lie because they are oblivious and not aware of the results and effects of lying over time. What could be so damaging in telling a lie? Nothing more than a defective character, a lost trust, missed opportunities, a degradation of morality, embarrassment, and failure. If you've used a lie here and there, in order to look good in front of people, then you need to tell the truth. People will always respect you more for an assumed mistake, but never for a permitted lie.

There is an enormous difference between an intelligent person and a credible one. Intelligent people impress, while the credible ones, influence. Credibility doesn't come only as a result of integrity. In which category do you want to be? Integrity is a discipline, not a talent. It is a choice. It's the choice of being honest, truthful and correct in any circumstance of life.

Unfortunately, in today's society, integrity is neither looked for nor glorified for its true value, that's why people constantly fail. We have all kinds of examples of people who reached the top of the mountain through deceiving (lack of integrity). But what they, don't realize is that they may reach the top of the mountain, but it's just a matter of time before they fall. If the foundation is not good, nor will be the lasting of the construction.

Ask yourself what kind of person you want to be, upright or compromised? No matter what you choose, keep in mind the truth which your choice reflects.

2) Responsibility

Rabindranath Tagore said: "I slept and dreamed that life was happiness. I woke up and realized that life was a duty. I did my duty and then happiness came ". A happy and fulfilled life begins with responsibility. Unfortunately, lack of responsibility is an international sport that we all tend to practice, both in our social life, as well as in the private one.

A child permanently transmits to his parents a clear message: "I totally depend on you. I can't do anything alone, even if I try. I can't assume the consequences of my decisions. In the end, I'm just a kid". Later, somewhere at 14 years old, when he grows up, the message is changed completely. It sounds like this: "Why can't you leave me in peace?!"

I want to be independent. I don't want to be told what to do. I want to decide for myself, but the results of my decisions have to be solved by you, because I am not responsible for the consequences, only for the decisions. When reaching maturity, things are more complex, but at the same time, they are a combination between "totally dependent on yourself" and "totally independent". They become: "You can count on me to" which is really the quality of a person's adult character.

No matter how bizarre it may seem, there are still elderly people who act as kids. Unfortunately, they are all around us. Very few are willing to assume total responsibility for what happens to them. The good news is that any of us can be part of this category. Accepting responsibility, even if others run from it, means to put yourself above all. In this way, the chances of a successful career, of finding a job, starting a stable relationship are far higher.

The one who accepts responsibility at his workplace manages to obtain the highest position. The one who accepts responsibility in society becomes the leader. Winston Churchill said: "Responsibility is the price of greatness". How high you want to get and how much you'll succeed is due to the responsibility you assume.

Becoming a responsible person means accepting the consequences, and looking at yourself as being the source of each thing that happens to you, continuing to fight despite hard times, prejudices and all the negative things that have happened or that are currently happening, in other words, to assume your destiny. Other people's choices can affect you only if you allow them. Responsibility also means accepting that you and only you are responsible for every past or present experience that you're the sole guilty party for what happened in the past, for what is happening in the present and for what will happen in the future. Responsibility has to do with choices: choosing to accept and change your life or choosing to deny and remain the same.

The number one enemy of responsibility is the excuse: "I'm not responsible because...". Those who don't want to assume responsibility have an excuse for anything that happened to them or for everything that they are accused of the blame must be put on God, a friend, bad weather, car, tough luck, destiny, the devil, back pain, family, the place where they are located, poverty. "I'm not the one to blame for the boredom that I experience, it's the bad weather." "I'm not to blame for the poor outcome of my relationship, heading towards divorce, but (she) he is to blame." "I'm not to blame for the extra pounds I've gained, but the company that produces unhealthy food." "I'm not to blame for the failure of the organization. The workers are to blame because they don't give their whole interest." "I'm not to blame for our arguing and for the rupture that occurred between us, but he is with his narrow thinking." "I am not to blame for wasting my life, I haven't done anything meaningful because of the family in which I was born, the bad luck that I've had, my destiny, my faith...", "I am not to blame for my financial situation and my debts. My small salary is to blame, as it doesn't cover all my expenses." "I'm not to blame because I'm late. The car or the person after I've waited for is to blame, the shower which broke down, the phone that did not work..." Excuses after excuses, after excuses. Excuses bring to light the crack in the character, and the conclusion is only one: that person is irresponsible.

Allow me to ask you, when have you agreed to assume responsibility and when did you say something to this effect? Or more specifically, when was the last time when you invoked an excuse? We are extremely frustrated when the phone which was supposed to ring failed to do so, and the one who was supposed to contact us, apparently forgot. We become frustrated when the plane that was supposed to take off is still late. We always complain about others, but when we do these things, we find excuses.

The problem with excuses is that once used, the brain stops processing. If you invoke an excuse, your brain has received the definition needed to define the thing that happened. Do you recall what I've emphasized in the previous chapters? The brain can't "close" information until it receives an image, a definition. Once the definition has been received, the brain will cease to look for a way out of that situation. No matter how simple or complicated a thing that happened might be, the brain will find a way to get out of the impasse, but with one condition: to admit that you're responsible for what happened. When responsibility is assumed, the brain is compelled to search for the solution.

Let's assume that your company experiences a massive loss, either due to the choices made, of purchasing, or even the marketplace which you depend on. No matter on what side the ball is, you should never dismiss the responsibility. Even if the market is the one that produced the loss, you are the one responsible for searching a solution in order to put the company back on its feet. Even if your business partner is guilty of the loss, you're responsible for associating with him. Keep staying responsible, not in order to find a solution. By doing so and demanding your employees contribute to solving the situation, the solution will come.

Accept responsibility regarding your own life and then it will truly change. As long as you act like a victim, you will not become responsible for what is happening. But when you understand that you are responsible, you will begin to change the world. I want to help you become responsible for everything that happens in your life. Any state, emotion, and experiences are created by you. You are the one who decides how to act and the state which you adopt in every circumstance. From now on, develop this component of your character, so that, whatever is happening around you, you'll stay strong, happy and with a smile on your face. Even if all around you are negative, you must stay positive, having the attitude that nothing is impossible. The day you choose responsibility is the day you reach the level of maturity.

Samuel B. Fuller is an example of assumed responsibility. Born in Louisiana (USA), in a poor family of black farmers, with seven children and decreased financial possibilities, he began working at the age of five. In the sixth grade, due to poverty, he was forced to permanently give up school. At the age of nine, he became a skilled sales person, selling various products door to door. Although he grew up in a community of people without education, Fuller had an advantage that nobody else around him had: a remarkable mother, who refused to accept poverty as a lifestyle. She knew that their limited means was not everything that life had to offer, despite the fact that those in the community accepted this life. For her, it was impossible that God almighty and strong, who placed them in a prosperous society could have only that plan for them. Therefore, she used to talk to the little Samuel about her dreams: "We should not be poor. Never say that God's will for us is to be poor. We are poor not because of God, but because your father and others from our family accepted poverty as a lifestyle, without wanting to live differently."

This idea was repeated again and again and became a belief that little Fuller developed over the years. Although those around him got used to the situation, he began to wish for prosperity. Persuaded by his mother's words, he began selling soap door to door for a period of twelve years, until one day, he received the news that the company which supplied him would be sold for $125 000.

Upon receiving this news, he went immediately to the seller with an offer to purchase it but had a problem: in all twelve years of work, he had no more than $25 000. He made a deposit of the whole sum, signing a contract that obliged him to gather the remaining amount within 10 days. Otherwise, he would lose all the money he gathered and along with that, his twelve years of work. Immediately after signing the contract, Samuel went from business to business, to those to whom he'd sold soap for a long time, to ask for a loan. With help from friends and from companies, he reached the sum of $115.000 by the ninth day. However, he still lacked $10.000.

In the last evening, while thinking how to continue further, he said: "I tried in every place I could, but still, I don't have enough money". Then, in his room, he bowed on his knees and prayed: "God, please guide me to the person that will lend me 10.000 dollars, the difference I need." He explains s what happened next: "I prayed and asked God for a sign. I told him that I would walk down the street until I found a light on at a business and I would go there to ask for money. This was the sign that I asked from God."

At 11 o'clock in the evening, Samuel Fuller went down on the 61st street, until, a few blocks away, he saw a light in a contractor's office. He entered and saw a man exhausted from work. Full of confidence, Fuller entered and asked him if he wanted to make a thousand dollars. The man quickly replied: "Of course I want to!" Then Samuel asked for a loan of 10.000 dollars and told him that he will be obliged by contract to return the sum with $1000 dollars interest. He told him in detail about the company he wanted to buy and about everybody else who lent him money. That evening he left the office with 10.000 dollars and purchased the company, in addition to which he received a percentage of another 7 companies.

He became so prosperous that he was called the richest African-American. Asked later, what was the secret to success, he said: "We are poor not because of God, but due to the fact that our father did not develop the desire to prosper. I ended up where I am because I knew what I wanted. I had a dream as an objective, the Bible for meditation, and several books for inspiration. "

Samuel B. Fuller is an example of what assuming responsibility means. Don't forget that you're not poor because of God, but because you didn't take the chance to change what you're experiencing today. If you blame God, your poor family, the environment, the country where you were born or whatever, you'll never get out your current situation, and you will live limited and frustrated for the rest of your life. Successful people don't believe in excuses because they're the engineers of their own lives. They do not invoke excuses for their inability, don't put the blame on the failures, nor do they blame others beside themselves. Successful people take individual decisions for their own lives. Are you such a person?

Let me ask you if you're one of the "excuse people". If yes, then you need to get rid of any kind of excuse and become responsible. You and only you are responsible. You must convince yourself that there are no excuses in life. A mature man doesn't seek excuses and because you want to become such a person, you must decide starting from this moment: "From now on, I'm done with excuses! Responsibility is the quality that I have. My character reflects RESPONSIBILITY." Assuming responsibilities for everything you experience in life is the highest form of maturity that anyone can achieve.

3) Attitude

Every day that we live, any circumstance we face depends on us, and with what attitude we want to move forward. This is what determines the experiences that we have. Only 10% represents what happens in reality with us, the remaining 90% is our answer. Each of us is responsible for his attitude, that is, the adopted position in any situation. A very good belief responds to attitude will lead to great choices.

Attitude influences the opinion of those surrounding us and dictates the acceptance or rejection of the place of employment for which we applied, the career we want, success or failure. Attitude is the mirror of a person's choices.

Carnegie Institute conducted a study on 10,000 successful people, concluding that 15% of their success was due to training, while the remaining 85% percent is due to character. The feature identified by the Institute was the attitude which really decides what we see and how we coordinate what we feel. Psychologists say that we see what we are prepared to see, meaning that we respond to our beliefs. What we choose to feel determines our attitude. Unfortunately, many of us allow our attitude to be influenced by the emotions we feel, instead of letting the attitude coordinate the emotions that we feel. It is unlikely for a person who has a poor attitude to prevail. The attitude either propels or stops you.

The attitude that we adopt in each circumstance is determined by two opposite factors, which constantly battle. These factors are the possible and the impossible. While the possible motivates, encourages, and brings you an advantage, the impossible pulls you back, limits and brings disadvantages. The impossible has as an excuse the expression, "It can't be done." How many people around you have you seen with an impossible attitude? There is no point in trying, you're wasting your time, others tried and failed, I can't, I have no potential, I don't have what I need in order to succeed, I am not smart enough, I am not capable. They are so negative, that for every dream, aspiration, hope, wish have a reason for not success.

Are you such a person? Hopefully not, but if you are, then you immediately need to get rid of this attitude, because what you think, will be what you do. If you think that it is impossible, it will be impossible, if you think that is possible, it will be possible. You decide if it can be done or not.

On every street corner, you see people who fail to assume the responsibilities they have as a result of their choices. They prefer to blame anything or anyone except them. Fate, the environment, bad luck, the family in which they were born, people around them led them to bankruptcy. These people have the wrong attitude regarding the problems they have created themselves. The most important day of our lives is the one we assume responsibility for our own attitude. This is the day we choose, growth maturity and success. God is the one who decides what we go through in life, but we are the ones who choose how we go through it. Each choice requires an attitude, an attitude is what separates us from the mediocre people. Changing attitudes depends on:

- Beliefs - choices are based on beliefs you have as to how you should react in a certain moment;
- Habits - are the way you manifest beliefs on the outside, meaning your behavior.
- The emotional state - what you feel inside expressed through the attitude you reflect on the outside

If you want to change your attitude, make sure that you have good beliefs and habits and that you're in control of your emotional states, with regards to what you feel. According to the example given in the previous chapters, replace negative habits and beliefs with positive ones and you'll reflect a positive attitude. Significantly improving your attitude means that, although you can't change the world around you, you can change the world that you perceive inside. Outside change comes from the inside. Once the interior world is changed, it will show on the outside.

At all times, altitude determines attitude. The maximum point you'll reach in life depends on your attitude.

Example: Sir John Templeton, a famous multi-billionaire, started from scratch in life. Born into a modest, very poor family, lacking financial possibilities, he decided at one point, in his youth, to take responsibility for the life that stood before him. He ceased to blame his destiny, family, circumstances and decided to take his life into his own hands. He was firmly determined to become not only financially stable but also prosperous so that others could benefit from his prosperity.

Templeton launched himself financially during an extremely difficult period of the 30s, during the great economic depression in the United States. His motto was: "Pessimism is the secret of success". He made money in a time when those around him were so pessimistic and desperate that they sold their business, homes, land. When Hitler invaded Europe, people panicked and tried to sell their properties, in order not to suffer losses. Then, Templeton invested all his money in order to purchase (sometimes even on a dollar) all the shops, restaurants, businesses and houses that were available at low prices. Within a few years, the economic market rectified, and Templeton retained all the properties. He continued to invest, this time in Japan, as the country crashed economically after the Second World War. He purchased well-priced properties which were expensive. Years later, when Japan relaunched, he began selling what he bought, obtaining a very high profit. He did the same in South America.

Templeton has left this world, but he left behind him a foundation called "The Templeton Fund" that invests a huge sum of money annually in helping people in need. He is recognized as one of the most generous people in history, delivering over $1 billion to charity. He explained that his success was due to taking responsibility seriously and controlling his feelings.

You and I decide what we will do with our lives. Success comes as a result of the attitude we adopt. Templeton could have been just as pessimistic as others around him, but he chose to remain optimistic. While others blamed the war, economy, market, he deliberately and responsibly chased change, a solution to the problem experienced worldwide. He found it and in this manner, he climbed the peaks of success.

4) Perseverance

Perseverance is a constant and means not giving up, no matter the circumstances around you. Perseverance determines if success will become a lifestyle or whether it remains only a dream. We all have abilities in solving things, but only the successful people finish what they start. A wise person will finish everything he starts.

Perseverance means keeping on going, even when everyone around you stops; it means moving forward, even if those around you go backward; it means to believe, even if others don't; it means to continue dreaming, even if others no longer do so. Perseverance is what separates you from the crowd.

In a course of resistance, all begins in force, full of confidence, but only those who persevere win in the end. It is important how you start, but success is determined by how you finish. In other words, success does not lie in the ability to start a thing, but the ability to finish what you've started.

Ernest Lantos Pam was a woman who was bored, sad, angry, and disappointed with life. Most of her time was spent in bed, without doing anything significant, until one day, she began to think about her personal development. One morning, she heard on the radio that in the city in which she lived, a new radio station was going to open. Full of enthusiasm, she went straight to the future radio station, in order to submit her CV, but the director told her that there was nothing available. Pam went down the hall, where she stayed all day long because she had "problems with hearing". She didn't go there to receive such a response, therefore, she did not want to hear it.

The next day she applied again for the job, but her hearing did not improve, because the answer was the same. Again, she went down the hall and waited. The third day she repeated the experience. After seeing how determined she was, the director announced to her that it was possible there was a job available for her. Since that time, Pam's hearing was restored. That was the only answer that she was willing to accept and which she received after three days of perseverance. She took the responsibilities of her new job and after a few weeks, she was already number one among all of those with experience. She helped grow of the company's profit by 400% and was appointed a manager.

Later, she traveled within America and taught people what it meant to persevere and not give up, especially when you are at a point in your life when nothing makes sense. Perseverance helps you rise, regardless of how many times you fall and to believe when you no longer see. It makes wonders.

Pam learned the lesson that Jesus taught His disciples. He talked about a woman that suffered an injustice and the judge was not willing to help her.

Despite this, the woman went each morning to the judge, again and again, and in the end, her wishes were listened to. The judge admitted that he was not afraid of people, but he was willing to bring her justice because she didn't give up.

When she went to the interview, Pam knew one thing: she either received the job or would keep on returning until she received it. She was determined not to give up under any circumstances.

The enemy of perseverance is renunciation. What do you do when you have tried over and over again, but nothing seems to happen? Do you give up or keep on going? Thomas Edison said: "Most of the time I use people's renounced ideas, the abandoned ones, which are not reconsidered". He managed to transform the ideas that others generated, but which they didn't choose to persevere with. What Pam had as a plus apart from other people was perseverance, which helped her go until she got what she wanted, even if that meant a thousand attempts.

During an interview, Edison was asked by a reporter what led him to continue trying so many times, without giving up. He said: "The reason I'm here now, talking to you is that I did what I've proposed to do. Otherwise, I would be in the workshop, trying another method, and another, until I succeeded." Perseverance will help you stay focused on your dream, despite surrounding turbulence.

The difference between people who succeed and those who fail is perseverance. Those who got it right, carried on right up to the end, while others were put down by renunciation. Failure does not exist, only methods that do not function. When you find yourself in a difficult position, remember that the solution is in you. If you've tried and it didn't work, try another strategy.

Success in life is defined by this component of the character called perseverance, but what makes the difference is perseverance plus strategy. It is not enough just to persevere, but it is important to have a correct strategy. If you pursue a while and nothing has changed, it is a sign that you should change your strategy. If you see that the method you try does not give results, change it.

The most beautiful definition for perseverance is presented by the most influential person that ever existed and it's written in the Bible: "Ask and you will be given, knock and it will open, seek and you will find". These three sentences represent perseverance plus strategy. In other words: ask and if you see that you don't receive an answer, modify your strategy of knocking. If you've knocked and seen that the door doesn't open, change your strategy again and seek. Jesus says to never give up and continue until you succeed.

Perseverance is the component that makes the difference in character. Without it, a character is incomplete. Any successful person credits his perseverance. As humans, we tend to renounce after the first attempt and this is the reason others don't manage to see their dream realized, although they have potential and possibilities as large as any other man. Adopt this component in your character, knowing that even though you have not yet managed to get where you've proposed, you're closer than yesterday. A river manages to dig in the stone not because of its power, but through perseverance.

Remember that life is a journey. If you received everything you wanted in a second, then it would no longer make sense to live it. Enjoy every moment, knowing that at the end, every moment you've persevered, renouncing the idea of giving up, brought you a step closer to success. The most beautiful and precious pearl is extracted through the perseverance of a clam, which continues to form it, despite the suffering and pain.

If you want to transform your dreams into rare and precious pearls, then you need to model your character in such a way, so that perseverance and all other components become your best friends, on whom you can rely in any situation. Today I'm closer than I was yesterday.

5) Courage

Courage is another extremely valuable item that any strong character should have. It does not necessarily mean the absence of fear, but rather the power to master it. Fear is our number one enemy, which often prevents us from seeing beyond the circumstances. Each of us has two options: to take action based on courage or let ourselves be coordinated by fear. The one who is driven by fear becomes fearful, while the other who is coordinated by courage becomes brave. Courage is vital because it determines failure or success in every struggle.

Defined at the mind level, courage is nothing but the ability to control our thoughts. The person who can control their thoughts is brave, while the one who can't is fearful. Imagine, what might happen if you found yourself in a critical situation and don't know what to choose? You would lose control of your thoughts and take action driven by fear, or you would control your thoughts and take action full of courage. No matter how powerful you are on the outside, if courage is not a part of your character, you will lose every battle. It is courage which makes the difference in life. If you seed courage, you will form a strong character, if you seed fear, you'll have an unstable character. Courage means to find yourself in front of a problem and say with determination: I can fix it. Courage means to renounce any negative thoughts that arise in your mind (I'll never reach success, I am not prepared enough, I lack the necessary abilities, etc.) and transform them into positive ones.

A lost battle at thought level will lead to cowardliness and failure, while a won battle will lead to courage and success. Why do we fail? Because we do not have enough courage. Choices resulting from fear will always limit us, but choices resulting from courage will propel us forward. Those who have accomplished something great are those who defeated their fear. Their potential was released.

An important component resulting from courage is perseverance, which always makes the difference. As long as courage exists, motivation will come and push you into persevering, and persevering brings victory. A brave person is the one who perseveres until he accomplishes everything that he wants. Perseverance produces long-term results, but it comes in the wake of courage. If you do not believe that you can succeed, you will be afraid and won't persevere. Nothing in the world can replace courage. Neither talent, money, influence, nor education. Nothing is more common in this world than talented people without success.

Courage leads to perseverance and determination. If you're a person who loses the fights at the level of thoughts, then you need the courage to sidestep any fear. Start from this point on to replace the fears inside with courage, with perseverance, determination and you will no longer experience failure. Each time you fall, you will be even more determined. When all give up you must keep on going.

Robert Schuller says: "Incredible people are just ordinary people, with an incredible level of determination".

Life brings challenges daily, but despite problems and difficulties, it's not what happens to us that is important, but what we do with what happens to us. This will decide where we'll end up.

Rosa Parks was a simple, African-American woman, who changed history and the whole world with a single act of courage. Acting on behalf of human rights, Rosa was arrested on 1st December 1955, in Montgomery, Alabama, for refusing to give up her seat on a bus to a white person. She decided not to accept fear as a lifestyle and chose to speak freely about her desires. Courage enabled her to oppose the laws that established inferior rights for black people, and this meant freedom and justice for many citizens. Her act of courage became the symbol of the civil rights movement, lead by Martin Luther King and resulted in gaining equal rights for everyone. In her elderly years, this woman received honors and medals for her bravery and a statue was built in her memory. She was the first woman who had an official ceremony in the U.S. Capitol.

Rosa Parks has left this world, but left a symbol that will remain forever in history: courage. Maybe you're a person who resembles Rosa Parks. You know what you need to do in order to follow your dream, career or ideals, but you're afraid of what might happen during the process.

You know that you should banish your fears and speak freely about what you believe, but you're afraid of other's opinions. You know how your life will change if you overcome fear and submit your CV to the company that you've always dreamt of working for, but the fear of rejection paralyzes you.

You know you like that person, but the fear of receiving a "no" pulls you back. Fears appear in many forms, but they all have one thing in common: limitation. Choose to overcome your fears and listen to God's calling.

6) *Flexibility*

It's another component of a strong character, which is expressed through humor and sensitivity. A flexible person knows when to smile and when to cry, when to be hilarious and when to be serious. Flexibility has to do with emotions. A man who owns his emotions is a happy man, while a man who is controlled by emotions is an unhappy man. You and I have the power to choose what, when, and how to feel. I am amazed by the number of people who are overwhelmed by a certain emotion, believing that this makes him great. The best boss is not the one that poses as a serious person, neither the one who acts hilarious, but the one who knows how to relate to each circumstance. A leader, a teacher, a friend, a partner, a successful parent must know how and when to express a certain kind of emotion.

The enemy of flexibility is rigidity, meaning the incapacity to relate to situations depending on the environment, time, place, and person. Instead, flexibility means to have the right emotion, at the right time. A rigid person is the one who lives in the past. He is always one step behind. These kind of people are unhappy because they seek to live the present in the past, which is impossible. It is unwise to try living today what you've experienced yesterday because yesterday is not today and today is not yesterday. You find yourself in a new day with new challenges, which will manage to control you, not vice-versa. In each day of our lives, God creates extremely beautiful moments, which, when emphasized, make the difference. The secret of a beautiful life is not obtaining the job you want, but the joy and satisfaction that you extract from each successful day towards accomplishment. Many of us think that if we had that thing, we would be happier until we obtain that particular thing and wake up and see that nothing has changed.

Don't seek happiness in fulfilling a thing or a dream, although this should be an aspiration. On the contrary, search for it in the beautiful moments, on the road to success.

Are you that person who knows how to enjoy every moment, or are you the kind of rigid person who believes smiling means weakness? For a long period of time, people believed that being rigid and serious all the time was a proof of leadership. The reality is different. A true leader knows when to be smiley and even to joke, but at the same time, knows when to keep his dignity and seriousness. If you are a leader and try to do something that doesn't fit you, that is, trying to act serious, then, in fact, you're a dictator and people around you will want nothing to do with you.

God gave a sensitive side to each character because in this way we can free ourselves of all the accumulated tension. At the same time, he gave us a joyful side from which we take our positivity. Used wisely, the two will make a perfect combination, called flexibility and pliability.

Being flexible also means understanding that we are in a continuous transformation. Nobody is perfect and nobody knows everything; that's why flexibility is an extremely important feature in the era in which we live. A strong character is not the one who runs away from change, but the one that is in a continuous process of modeling. Learning and shaping is a process which takes place until we die if we haven't decided we know enough, so we no longer need change.

Being more flexible means adapting to the changes around you, no matter what position others adopt. The most successful people are those who understand that the transition is real and have adapted immediately. The other category, in contrast, waited and hoped that it would be the same as before, but came to discover that it would never be the same. Unfortunately, their observation came much too late. If you truly want to succeed in life, then you need to make a decision for you.

Regardless of the location, forced or deliberately, I choose to go, I will take advantage of the smallest detail that I can extract. Although it's not the place where I see myself for the rest of my life, it's the place where I am now, so I will not allow my feelings to produce negative thoughts and make my stay an ordeal. Learn now how to enjoy the smallest things, and when you get to the big ones, you will know how to appreciate them. Smile, regardless of the day, because only you can decide how each day will end up. Learn to feel with those who feel and enjoy with those who enjoy themselves. Being flexible means to be like a tree: when the wind blows, you move slightly in his direction, but never change your values and your fixed position; when it rains, enjoy the coolness and humidity that it offers and develop yourself; when it's drought, use the reserve that you've accumulated during the rain. A strong character is a graceful one who is in continuous development.

Bethany Hamilton was a girl with big dreams, being passionate about surf. Her desire was to win the competitions she attended. But everything was shattered on 31 of October 2003, during a workout in which she lost her left arm as a result of a shark attack. She was only 13 years old. Although on the way to the hospital, she lost approximately 60% of the total quantity of blood, she managed to survive. Her dream was shattered, but not for long. Without an arm, but with a positive attitude, she resumed surfing and managed to win competition after competition, just as before. Her belief in herself and God led her towards success. Following the accident, and until 2014, she finished in first place, six times and second and third place numerous times. She wrote a book called "Soul Surfer", which resulted in a movie in 2011.

Today, Bethany is married, has a child, and enjoys her family. She managed to get over her suffering and demonstrated that problems are temporary for those who know how to adopt a correct attitude and to be more versatile. In life, we will often pass through moments where we're going to be challenged, but it's up to us if we decide to overcome difficulties, turning them into opportunities. Flexibility means knowing how to enjoy each thing, in every moment.

7) Patience

Patience means acting in an appropriate manner, at the right time and moment; it means to know how to control time. Time can be the cruel enemy of a person, but also his best friend, depending on the way it's harnessed and used. Patience is a quality that every powerful character must learn. Every successful person, who managed to win the fight with time, passed through this process until he was prepared. God uses time to shape our character, helping us replace, little by little, the negative things, with positive ones. Thus, with the passing of time, we become more wise and responsible. This is not a rule that applies to everyone, but the one who perseveres becomes wiser with the passing of each day.

Just as the most expensive wood, metal or paintings are the older ones, so is character formed over time. Time will bring to light everything that is best, but with the condition to get started now. Most people are just as irresponsible at 80 years as they were in their youth, because they believed that time helps them grow, which is untrue. Maturity comes after taking responsibilities. Patience helps us persevere and continue our path to success. Even a habit you want to change takes 30 days until it is totally replaced. Overnight success is a lie and nobody has ever experienced it. Not even the "lucky" one who won at bingo, because his earnings implied the decision to purchase a ticket, to write and wait for the outcome of the game.

No matter at what point you are in life, it is important to know one thing: time can be the cruel enemy and can sabotage you, or may be your best friend and help you achieve success. You decide what you'll do with it. If you use it irresponsibly and without a plan, it becomes your number one enemy, if you use it as a well-defined plan, together with assuming responsibility, it will drive you to the top of the mountain. A saying says: "If you fail to plan, then plan to fail". Manage your time correctly and be patient, because the results will be unbelievable. What is important is that all this time, you enjoy every moment. Don't expect success overnight in order to be happy, because it is possible that, once there, you may not have time do so.

A child isn't born a runner, but in order to become one, he must go through a process, step by step. First, he learns to crawl after which he slowly makes the first steps. Then, he barely starts to slowly run and develop until running becomes increasingly easy.

The main enemy of time is a rush. A proverb says: "Rushing spoils the job". Don't rush into answering, until you have the answer. Continue to analyze and observe, until you find the best answer. Don't rush into judging, until you know the reason behind the problem. Assimilate patience as a component of your character. Develop a principle that helps you stay calm, no matter of other's precipitation.

The best decisions are the analyzed and verified ones. Now it's the perfect moment to decide to make time. Benjamin Franklin is the one who said: "Time means money". Lost time means lost money and lost money means problems. The right time is not "now", but it's when "I'm ready". Decide that you will never give up, no matter how much it will take to succeed. Decide that despite the fact that others waste time, you'll exploit and use it wisely.

8) Fidelity

Although last on the list of the character's components, fidelity is just as important, if not even more important. Fidelity is a word that, for most, does not mean very much, but its benefits are priceless. Have you ever wondered what results loyalty could sustain in your career? After making observations, I realized that more than anything, in the objective of attainment, there is a need for fidelity. For sure, courage, attitude, integrity, perseverance, patience, and fidelity have their importance, but more important than all of these is to stay faithful to that career or dream. Remaining loyal to your dream means determining yourself to discover the path in that direction. Even if things are not going as you've imagined, stay faithful, because you know that this is God's will for your life.

The world would be happier if people would appreciate this component of the character, called fidelity. I can't leave the company, place of employment, business partner, just because things don't work as they used to. A loyal person knows that part of his responsibility is to stay together with the others in both glory, unity, and disappointment. I am not allowed to leave my relationship just because it no longer works as it used to. Your responsibility is to stay loyal to your partner, no matter if you experience rainy or sunny seasons. The good part is that each season you can enjoy one another, but only if you're determined to stay loyal. We all start all sorts of things, but only those who stay loyal until the end will enjoy the harvest.

Fidelity is the ability to remain faithful or loyal following a choice. Without loyalty towards that dream, you will always remain just a visitor. Without loyalty towards that business, you'll end up being sabotaged. Without loyalty towards your partner, you'll end up in disappointment.

The enemy of fidelity is infidelity, which has produced and continues to produce the biggest conflicts and problems until today. Families are assaulted daily by the trap called infidelity.

Infidelity knows no boundaries, backgrounds, culture, or age. The business, economy, relationships suffer due to infidelity. You will suffer from infidelity if you let it into your character. In any area of the society you're going to enter, intend to or are already in, fidelity is on the top of the list (of employers, partners, investors). Employers require fidelity from employees because they know that their dedication influences the well-being of the company. Any person who dreams of the right partner searches for this component called fidelity because he knows that the person will remain faithful no matter the ups or downs.

Finally, there is one person who needs fidelity in his development process more than anything else. Success or failure is determined by how faithful it will be to his life. That person is you. Yes, you need fidelity more than anything. To remain loyal to yourself means to fulfill your obligations towards yourself and one of them is shaping a strong and stable character. If you remain faithful to your own person, meaning your values, beliefs, habits and principles, then you will also remain faithful to your partner, career, dreams, friends, and last but, not least, to the life you live now. Choose to stay faithful to you and to God's calling.

The benefits of a transformed character

A strong character is more valuable than gold. Never can gold buy a character, but a character can, at any time buy gold. Nothing can be compared with a developed character. If you understand the importance of character, then you will experience all the wonderful things resulting from success.

Turn your character into the reason you will succeed. If you do not experience the success you're dreaming of, the career you wish for and success that you've proposed, then you should put a question mark over your character. Choices, actions, beliefs, and habits are all related to character. Choose at this very moment to reevaluate the character you've developed up to this time. If you have never done this and evaluated the results it produces in your life, you'll probably feel the same way I did when I realized that no matter how much I was struggling to succeed, I wasn't making any progress because of the minuses in my character.

If you recognize yourself in what I'm saying, it means that you are part of the vast category of those who formed their character from the way they relate to the circumstances. The good part is that you always have a choice to make, regardless of the situation, but you'll never choose differently from who you are. What you should know, however, is that your family, friends, school and culture formed your personality before you had the opportunity to take your life into your own hands. Before you decided what you'd do, they've already decided for you, perhaps indirectly, what, how, and how much you will be able to achieve. In other words, what you are today is due to the limits that were imposed and that controlled your entire life. Knowing this, you're not cleared of the accountability to create a different kind of life, but rather obliged by the decision that is in front of you.

Decide that, starting from now, you must change your future by choosing the most expensive and valuable thing in the universe, called discipline. Discipline is the chisel that each of us should have. Your life is on the verge of becoming a piece of art, but you must take the chisel called discipline and use it on your character.

Discipline means character, and character means success.

You're probably wondering, "What are the benefits of a transformed character"? I want to give you just a few of the many kinds of benefits you will have:

- Character saves your business, place of employment and career from the trap called a lie, offering in return the pleasure of doing what you love.
- Character saves your marriage from the trap called infidelity, offering in return the company and happiness of an extraordinary family.

- Character saves your life from the trap called limitation, offering instead the joy of accomplishing the things you've dreamed of.• Character saves your life from the trap called excuses, offering instead the result of a responsible life.
- Character saves your life from the trap called offering instead, the pleasure of using time as you desire.
- Character saves your life from the trap called fear, offering instead the benefits of courage.
- Character saves your life from the trap called negativity, giving you in return the pleasure of experiencing positivity.
- Character saves your life from the trap called rigidity, offering you the freedom of experiencing flexibility.
- Character saves your life from the trap called renunciation, giving you the pleasure of experiencing success.

You have whatever it takes to experience these things. God has blessed you with gifts and talents, with incredible and unique abilities, and your part is to free the potential hiding inside you. Your potential is limited because of your character, but once the character is changed, your potential will be freed and you will take control of your thoughts, beliefs, and habits and will become a person of character. Integrity will put you above those who not only lie to those around them, but also to themselves. Attitude will help you choose wisely in any circumstance, regardless of the difficulties which will appear. Courage will propel you forward, towards success, and even when all around you are limiting themselves and giving up, you will continue to firmly persevere until the end. Identify the fear and strengthen those sides of your personality which are not so strong.

How to strengthen your character
The first step in forming a strong character is to accept that you need a change in character. If you've accepted that a change is required, you need to go further and identify those components from your character that pull you down. To identify them, analyze your choices. These are the exterior mirrors of the character. To discover the cracks, I suggest two things:

1) On a sheet of paper that you will carry with you the following week, write the word: character, then watch the choices that you take. Write them immediately on a sheet of paper and at the end of the week, review them, establishing which components of character produced them.

2) Choose three friends you trust and tell them to describe everything that attracts them to you and every single thing that they dislike. Ask them to be open and honest in their presentation and be open to any feedback. At the end of their description, scan each thing they've told you, and if you think that they are right and honest in their presentation, accept it and start changing.

It is possible that the negatives you've accumulated may be caused by immature and irresponsible habits or your undeveloped personality. Whatever the cause, work at the transformation of the character to emphasize your true value created by God. Once the list is complete and you know what to change, use the chapter called "Change", for guidance.

11

Problems

Problems are those crucial moments that a person experiences in certain stages of life and it either strengthens or crushes them. Often, when we relate to problems, we think that we are less privileged than others. From our perspective, they do not experience the same situations, that's why they're so happy. The reality is that each of us experiences opposition in life, sooner or later. In such times, it is important to remind ourselves that these are inevitable. There are no more or less privileged people when it concerns difficulties. We all have our fair gain. The beauty is that difficulties give life meaning.

A wise philosopher said: "The only obstacle in a bird's path is the air which puts pressure on her flight, however, despite this, the air is the benefit through which the flight can be achieved". Without air, the bird would fall to the ground. The opposition is the condition for achieving the flight. So are the obstacles that we encounter in life. They are at the same time, a runway towards success. A life without oppositions significantly reduces someone's chance of escaping mediocrity.

Problems motivate us to discover and exceed ourselves. If you'll take a look into your life, you'll discover a list of things that you could never have realized, if you hadn't encountered those problems that emphasized something you didn't even know existed.

A study conducted on 300 people who changed the world, by means of the influence and impact they had (among those were Winston Churchill, Mahatma Gandhi, Albert Einstein, Abraham Lincoln, Nelson Mandela), shows that a quarter of them had a disability, and three-quarters were born in poverty, coming from poor or destroyed families in which there were serious tensions. What is the secret of these people's success, to whom no one gave a chance? They all had the same things in common: problems, obstacles, difficulties. These are issues that each of us encounters in life, but the difference between these 300 subjects and us, is that thing called attitude. While millions of people were kneed down by problems, these people raised above them, using them towards their growth

In any circumstance that life presents to us, the way we relate to situations belongs to us. But what we must know is that the choice we make determines our future experiences. The secret of success is related to attitude. Those 300 were people with attitude, chose to refuse the excuses that people invoked daily, in order to justify their wrong choices. They took the stones that blocked their path used them in the construction of a road. Unfortunately, many build a wall with these stones which blocks their path.

Problems can slow you down temporarily, but you are the only one who can stop them. There are no problems and obstacles that cannot be resolved. Attitude and perseverance will transform any problem into a step towards success. John Maxwell said: "The size of a problem is less important than the size of a person". If you're a strong person with a strong attitude, then whatever the extent of the problem, it will be just a temporary obstacle, which stands ready to be used towards strengthening your character. God allows certain circumstances in our life that guides our character towards its calling. The Bible encourages those who pass through difficulties to enjoy it because every difficulty produces fruit. This truth can be seen in every person's experiences.

How do you react when problems come? The attitude you adopt will determine the choice you make. In solving any problem, we need two things: a good attitude and a good choice. For positive results, you must understand the following truth: failure does not exist. Failure is just a definition that we unconsciously give to anything that we fail to do as we wanted. Believing in failure is a poison that destroys our dreams, affects our thoughts, and influences our decisions.

Fear of failure is one of the most frequently encountered features of mediocre people. If you're afraid of failure, then you will never be motivated to think creatively and act, because fear will bombard you with all sorts of negative thoughts that will block your success. Fear of failure means the highest level of negativity. It will make you believe that if you act you have all the chances to fail, that you're going to look ridiculous, will lose and those around you will laugh.

If you hugely desire that place of employment, you'll never have it if you take into account the possibility of failure. Although you like that girl or boy, you'll never have the courage to interact because you are afraid of rejection, meaning failure. If you have a big dream, you'll never be motivated enough to follow it, if you think of failure. Let me ask you what would you do if you knew that it is impossible to fail? Wouldn't everything change? If you believe that there's no chance for you to fail, you'll try again and again, until you find the method of making your wish come true.

The good news is that failure does not exist. It is just a myth, an imagination that arises in the mind, a fear. There are methods and results that don't fit or function, but not failure. Maybe things didn't turn out as you imagined, but this means that you've got a result you can change at any time. All you have to do is act differently, to get a different result. Eliminate from your dictionary the word "failure" and replace it with the word "result".

Each trial is an outcome, even if it's not the one that you wanted. Continue to change the way you act, until you get the right result. In order to become a successful person, you need to convince yourself that difficulties and problems are precisely the reason you will succeed. Many people see difficulties and problems as a failure when in fact, they are nothing else but challenges. Used correctly, difficulties and problems will make us stronger and more confident.

Problems are a choice

1) On what do we focus?

Whatever the things you choose to focus on, you'll feel them in your life. For example: if you focus on all unfair things that others or life did to you, then you'll feel horrible. If instead, you focus on all beautiful things, all opportunities that come your way, like the invitation that someone offered you, a job, the fact that you've met your life partner, or that you avoided an accident, that you went to that wonderful place, etc., you will create a positive impact on your emotions and choices. You are influenced by what you focus on; if you focus on people's mistakes and their carelessness, you will search for reasons they don't care and you'll find them everywhere; if you focus on people's qualities and their beauty, you'll find, positive, honest, forthcoming people at every step. Jesus said in the Gospel of Matthew: "Search and you will find". What you search for, that's what you'll find. The question is: are you aware of the importance of choices and the things you choose to focus on? A different life comes as a result of different choices.

2) What do the circumstances I pass through mean?

The questions we ask ourselves to determine the meaning we give a particular circumstance, that's why you must stop asking yourself meaningful questions, such as: "Why me? Why does everything happen only to me?" By contrast, ask yourself for example: "What does God want to teach me from this circumstance? What benefits will I have? How can I turn this problem into an opportunity? What is good in this?"

Most problems are not what they seem, so that's why questions will lead to their true meaning.

When you go through difficulties, you should always ask yourself, "What does the event mean?" Think about the experience that you've gone through, and the part on which you've focused your attention and as a result, determined what it means for you. For example, you have established that you were mistreated; that no one loves you; that someone

141

is trying to make a profit from you etc., depending on the conclusions you've reached, some feeling will arise inside you, which will urge you to act. The economy is falling, the business no longer functions the same, and you are worried and don't know what to do: to give up and become bankrupt, or to take advantage of this and start reinventing, changing and improving your business. You look and find an answer, you apply it and discover that it takes an unexpected turn. It can bring you into a position that you could have never achieved if there wasn't a crisis to provoke you to step forward and become creative. The relationship between you and your friend is going through a rough time and you don't know how to relate to him. You worry, quit, and you separate. But there is another version: take advantage of this situation and seek to strengthen the relationship, making it stronger and better.

You look at the relationship in which you are and at the crisis, asking yourself why things don't go as they should. What can you change? What could you do better? You come up with an answer, you apply it and the relationship takes a radical turn. It is mandatory that you ask yourself in any situation: is this the end, or the beginning? You determine the answer, you are the one who will come up with the conclusion. But I want to challenge you to meditate on the following topic: if you believe that this is the end, will you act as if this is the beginning? Will you have the same attitude as in the beginning? Will you be as enthusiastic, optimistic and creative? By contrast, you will observe there's no passion, you'll be stuck creatively, you will not find any solution, so you'll quit. If you or your spouse/husband, boyfriend/girlfriend think that you are at the end of your relationship, will you behave as if you were at its beginning? Certainly not! In fact, at the beginning, you were both so optimistic and creative, nothing stood in your way. The beautiful gestures full of imagination came naturally. The question is why? Because the relationship had another meaning to you, you viewed it differently. The brain will search for solutions as long as you decide to continue, but when you already came up with a conclusion, either positive or negative, it will stop searching, giving you what you chose. The meaning you give to the things you have experienced as a result of focus will affect your emotions, choices, and life.

3) What can we do?

The third thing we do following the choice on which we focus and the meaning we give to circumstances is to choose what we'll do, how we will act. Will you decide to give up because it is too much, or will you decide to continue fighting, to become stronger, more creative, wiser? What you decide will influence your actions.

What will you do if one day the doctor tells you that you have a tumor, or if you lose the one you love, or if you lose your business? Will you choose to focus on the negative part and ask yourself why you? Will you embitter yourself with ideas that life is unjust, that God might have prevented this from happening, or will you focus on those few things, although painful, that can make a difference and propel you straight ahead, instead of pulling you back?

Steve Jobs is known in history for his perseverance. Kicked out from his own company, Apple Computer, founded by means of a titanic work, Steve decided to focus on the positive side, which many of us don't have the power to see. He took advantage of it and founded a new company, called "Next", where Pixar was created (the digital animation program, which in a short period of time grew to be worth millions of dollars). Shortly after, the initial company, Apple Computer was required to buy this company. Steve came back and took over the company he founded, which at that time was on the verge of bankruptcy. He always searched for the positive side and thus managed to transform problems into opportunities. Because of this man who chose to focus on the positive things, you probably have an Apple device.

Don't forget that you can always choose between two things: positive and negative, pessimism and optimism. Your destiny is determined by your own decisions; what you choose to believe about yourself, about others, about God and society. They will affect all your life.

The questions we ask ourselves to determine the meaning we give to circumstances, therefore, do not ask "Why me?", "Why is this happening only to me?" On the contrary, ask yourself: "What does God want me to learn in this circumstance? What benefits will I have? How can I turn this problem into an opportunity?" Most problems are not what they seem, that's why questions will lead you to the true meaning of things. When everybody is desperate due to market and economy, instead of wondering why God set this disaster upon you, it is best to see what you can gain from this circumstance. By doing so, you'll become a Templeton, who despite the negativity and adversity of those surrounding him, became a millionaire. Such thinking helps you view challenges and take advantage of them.

When you are able to look at a problem and ask yourself what is good in it, then you truly are at another level, which will separate you from the crowd, from an economic, spiritual, material, or financial point of view. It takes a different kind of attitude, to be able to take advantage of every opportunity. But this means to see difficulties and problems as opportunities and not as problems. How you see them will determine what you will experience.

When you are struggling with problems, ask yourself:

- What can I learn from this problem?
- What is good in this problem?
- What should I do to transform this problem into an opportunity?
- What can I do to transform this problem according to the possibilities I have?
- How can I enjoy this problem, instead of crying?

All the questions above have the power to change circumstances into opportunities from which you can extract benefits. You may have been discovered with a serious disease and instead of panicking, you should ask yourself what good can come out of it? Will you stop smoking, begin eating healthily and exercise - meaning to change your lifestyle as you wanted, but so far haven't found the necessary motivation to do. Perhaps the disease becomes the motivation that you needed to win or succeed but never had.

Wilma Rudolph is an example who showed motivation resulting from opposition. She was prematurely born in 1940, in a family of 22 children resulting from two marriages. She was the 20th child. As Wilma grew up, she suffered numerous hospital internments and had to conquer her precarious health. In the end, she retained problems with her left leg and was forced to wear bandages and a form of a prosthesis. However, with great determination and the help of a therapeutic physician, she managed to stabilize her leg and pursue her dream of becoming a runner. In 1956, after hard work, she would become the first American female to win three gold medals in a single Olympics.

What is the obstacle that stands between you and your dream, between where you are and where you want to get? Whatever your answer is, one thing is certain: the same thing that blocks you today may become the reason for your success. You decide what your health problems, disabilities or accident you've suffered mean to you.

Glenn Verniss Cunningham turned the accident which he suffered into the reason for his success. Born on August 4, 1909, he was considered to be the greatest runner and athlete of all time. At the age of eight, he suffered an accident at school, because of a person who accidentally put gasoline instead of Calhoun in the canister. His brother, Floyd, just 13 years old, died from the fire, while he suffered serious burns to both legs.

Doctors predicted that he would no longer be able to walk, following the serious burns that burnt all the skin and flesh from his knees and all fingers of his left foot. They suggested leg amputation, but his parents refused. Two years after the accident, with a lot of determination and hours of work, he managed to gradually regain his ability to walk and later began to slowly run. With the belief that God would restore the power to walk and based on Isaiah 40:31 which says: "But those who put their trust in the Lord will renew their strength; they fly like eagles; run, but don't get tired, stray, and not tire", Glenn managed not only to walk again, but to run. He set record after record, won many medals and set three new world records, becoming one of the best runners of all time. Today, he is no longer alive, but a park in Kansas is named after him.

Glenn is an example showing that what happens to us as a result of someone's negligence should not stop us from continuing to dream and fulfill the calling that God gave us on this Earth. Whatever situation you are in now (the job that you missed, the CV that was rejected, etc.), don't give up and continue.

Jack Ma is the founder and executive director of the Alibaba's company, the largest online sales company in China. With a rated value estimated by Forbes magazine of 24.1 million dollars, he appears in the list of the most prosperous people in China. In 2004, in China, Jack was included in the top ten businessmen of the year, and in May 2009, he was named by Time magazine one of the 100 most influential people. In 2014, Forbes magazine puts him once again among the top 30 most powerful people in the world, while in the year 2015 he was honored with the award of the year, The Asian Awards. Also in 2015, Forbes named him the second richest man in China.

When you think of all these awards, you think of tremendous success and yet, the Jack Mak we know today was not always a prosperous and successful man. On the contrary, he grew up in the communist regime in China, he failed twice at the University exam, was refused at every place of employment to which he had applied, including KFC (Kentucky Fried Chicken). When the KFC company came to China, twenty people forwarded their resume, among them, was Jack Ma. Among these 20 people, 19 were accepted and only one was rejected, and that was Jack Ma.

The secret behind his success is defined by a single word, perseverance. As a teenager, he continued to persevere until he did something that would change his life forever. With each rejection, Jack stood up again and went ahead. The courage, determination, and perseverance lead him to success, although he never believed that he would be able to achieve.

Asked later, what was the catalyst that led him to where he is now, he declared: "The rejections! Each rejection that I experienced meant one more reason to continue." Because of the problems he encountered in the job search, today, he is famous. Tired of so many failed attempts, he decided to use the Internet from home, to waste time and forget about all the problems. But then he came up with a brilliant idea, which transformed him into what he is today.

He is not the only one who enjoys the services of his companies, but also millions of people that can use these services for various acquisitions.

God closed every door he tried to open, in order to help him get to the point of discovering this brilliant idea. Do you see how difficulties and opposition became the main reason for his success?

What problems and oppositions do you currently experience in your life and how would you define them? Are those the reason you quit or continue persevere, knowing that God will bring something good out of everything?

Maybe, following the car accident you've got a better car; perhaps due to the relationship that broke you were able to create another relationship better than the first one; perhaps due to the problems that your child has at school, you discovered that the school was not suitable for him; maybe the bankruptcy of your company opened up more profitable investments. Whatever you experience, it brings with it opportunities that will lead to unimaginable accomplishments, if you observe and take advantage of them.

Observe the problems and difficulties as opportunities. Tell yourself what you're not willing to do. Maybe you're not willing to give up every nice moment that you've experienced with your wife, just because at the moment the relationship is not in a good place. So, you'll search for the way of developing the relationship, taking advantage of this situation. You can discover what you did well and what you didn't, what worked and what hasn't worked and you are now determined not to give up the positive experience and every beautiful day that awaits in the future, just because you're experiencing a difficulty. On the contrary, you want to take advantage of the situation.

Julio Iglesias is the example of a crushed dream, but not a defeated one. He had a dream and a passion for which he fought in his youth, but his dream became unfeasible, when one day, he suffered a serious accident. His dream was to play professional soccer, which he did, for a short period of time.

In the early years of football, he played at Real Madrid Castilla, as a defender, but his career was shattered by a car accident where his spine was broken, his legs were weakened forever, requiring therapy for several years after the accident. For two years, he couldn't walk, so all he could to do was look as his football career shattered before his eyes. However, in the midst of these problems and difficulties which he has experienced, he stood up and began working on changing them into opportunities, launching in his future music career.

It all started when a nurse gave him a guitar to do something with his hands. From that moment, he began making another career, much greater than football, which led him to the list of the top best musical artists in history. In April 2013, he received two awards: the award for best and most popular international artist of all time in China. In his music career, he has won plenty of awards and recorded over 2600 Golden and platinum discs, becoming one of the most bought artists of all time.

Julio Iglesias managed to become known for his musical talent and success that led him to the peak of success. Moreover, he is the father of two other internationally known artists: Julio Iglesias and Junior Enrique Iglesias. This man understood that he could transform problems into opportunities. He could feel sorry for himself for the rest of his life and blame God, himself, the accident, the created problems. Still, he took advantage of a guitar and changed the problem into a musical career.

Maybe you're in this kind of impasse right now, or maybe you were, or will be at some point in the future. No matter where you are, it is important to understand that problems are only opportunities that can't wait to be recognized and used. If the dream you've had shattered in front of your eyes, without your being able to do anything, seek to find out of what you can make from this situation. Ask yourself what God wants from you because following that disappointment, you might discover just as Iglesias did, your true potential and talent, that once accessed, will take you much further than you would have ever managed in your dreams. God always works to our benefit, but we need to see His work and accept it, so we can take advantage of it.

You may suffer from a devastating disease or a financial loss. The question you should ask yourself is the following: "What is the good in that?" Don't focus on the negative things, because you will experience them as a result, but if you focus on the positive things, those will be the ones that you'll experience. Open your eyes and see problems as a source of growth.

The basic rule when you find yourself in a dead end is not to make any conclusions before you're sure that you have exhausted every other possibility. Once you come up with a definition of what that problem means, the brain stops searching for solutions. You choose how you're going to call every circumstance you go through. As problems are a choice, so is success, happiness, prosperity and your contribution. You decide how you're going to define each challenging moment.

Two people see the same thing but act differently. One uses it as a reason to take a step forward towards the implementation of his dream, the other uses it as a reason to take a step back and to give up on his dream. The difference is the name they chose to give to that thing. Name the difficult circumstances through which you pass as opportunities, not problems; opportunities to help you grow, develop, learn, avoid repetition, choose another method, become more motivated, more careful.

Successful people who changed the world by their influence and their achievements named them opportunities. People who didn't achieve too many meaningful things in life, call them problems. What do you call them? It is important to understand that the only problems that you've experienced so far, or will encounter from now on are those that you see as problems. You have chosen or will choose for problems to become problems, through the way you relate to them. I never have problems, because, for me, problems don't exist. Problems are opportunities.

12

Values

Your values are the standard of your behavior and how you define your way of doing things as correct and important for the lifestyle adopted. When your choices and actions are aligned with your values, then you'll feel fulfilled and cozy. You experience tranquility and peace of mind because you're comfortable in doing the right things in the right way. When choices and actions are not in line with your values, you feel unfulfilled, and your image is affected, for the things you value are not satisfied.

Each person chooses the values he prioritizes and which he transforms into a lifestyle. However, certain values must be respected regardless of the career, prestige, or name. These values are the moral ones, which we must adopt as our lifestyle. Values determine the value of a person because he always rises to the level of the adopted values. If you value the time in the company of wise people and well-prepared people, with influence in society, then you become such a person, with values similar to theirs. You have value, taking into account what you fructify.

The things you value are those beliefs that you've formed consciously or unconsciously. They are those priorities you've assumed and exploited more than anything; they are the most important things for you. Values determine priorities and progress. Based on the values you've assimilated, you verify if your life is heading towards what you imagined and hope you'll succeed.

When the things you do and how they're done fit with your values, you feel fulfilled and satisfied, but when these don't match with people's values you feel unsatisfied and unfulfilled.

Values exist, they're real and guide our life, so, it is important you identify them and set some goals for each of them. If you treasure family, but you're forced to work up to 50 hours per week, you will feel dissatisfied. In this case, the time spent with your family suffers. When you know what your values are, you can reshape your life and make decisions about how you choose to prioritize things. If you don't know, then you didn't form them consciously, but these formed themselves over time, resulting from the experiences you've had, both, good and bad. If every day, except when you work, you watch TV or are on social websites, this means that these are the things that you unconsciously fructify. The things you do reflect the values you have. If you have really good values, you will see that priorities are well defined by a plan applied daily. If you don't have well-defined values, it means that you're unconsciously doing things you don't even know you fructify.

Ask yourself: what are the things that you cultivate in life more than anything else? These are the beliefs and habits upon which you act. If you don't have well-defined values, I want to help you create them. In this way, you become disciplined and invest in important things on purpose, eliminating those which are less important. Why would you want to waste time with things that don't bring you any profit, when you could invest that time in things that you appreciate? If you don't create your own values, those around you will influence you and impose their own values. For example, if you enter into a circle of friends who gossip about everybody, or who waste time looking to the television, then it's not long until you will adopt the same habits. My desire is to help you develop your own values, to fructify them, so no matter what happens around you, you'll stay strong and with unbeatable values. Most people go along the River in the direction of the currents, unaware of the obstacles that will come and the losses they will suffer. You're reading this book because you don't want to be led by others. In this case, what are the most crucial things that you want to form as life principles or personal values?

To help you better understand, I wrote my own values in the order of my priorities:

a) God

b) Health

c) Family

d) Church

e) Dreams

f) Contribution

The order is established by the most important criteria. To be able to invest in myself, I must invest in my relationship with God. At such times, I grow level after level. Investing in my health, investing in the relationship with my wife and children, because it is impossible for an ill person to bring his contribution to the family, at the level of a healthy person. Investing in my relationship with God, in health and family, investing in the Church, because it's composed of strong and healthy families. You bring to church the investment and growth of the three domains of personal life. Investing in these four, I invest in my dreams. I motivate myself, I focus and dedicate myself to these dreams. Investing in these five, I bring my contribution into people's lives. We'll always influence those around us according to our growth and size. An influenced person will influence at a larger scale than others, but a less influenced person will influence people at the according level. If you truly want to contribute to our society, then invest in those five things which will determine the contribution to the lives of those around you.

What are the values that you've created for your life? If you are like the majority of the people, who didn't set clear values that help them guide their life, then it is easy to acknowledge why you didn't accomplish anything significant until this time. Success does not come by accident but needs to be well planned until you obtain results.

If you cannot itemize a few values that you're currently following, then you are a person who does what everybody does, trapped in a pattern and within the limits of others' standards. Still, the news is that you are not obliged to continue as you have until now, but now is the time to say "no more", to make a radical turn and build your life as you want to live it and not the one that others chose for you.

In order to change the values you've assimilated from the surrounding world, it would be good to firstly create a list of those that you want to implement from now on. Write on a sheet of paper in descending order, the most significant values you want to implement and that represent your priorities.

Seek to respect them daily, even if there are people or events that will distract your attention. Stick to your position no matter what, even if the ones around you lose their own values. Make a plan for each individual value. From where I stand, I know how I'm going to harness my relationship with God, health, Church, dreams, goals, and aspirations, and how will I harness the contribution that I make to people's lives. Below is how I see things:

God - What habits and beliefs do I create so that my relationship with God is harnessed daily? It can be a time spent in prayer and meditation or a study.

Health – What is my plan, through which I harness my health? It can be seven hours of sleep, healthy food, and workouts on some days of the week.

Family – What habits and beliefs do I lay down so that I harness my family daily? Maybe a time spend with the wife, with children, going out together, creative things, and surprises.

Church – What is my plan related to church? Maybe to participate in all programs, regardless of the need that the church has, offering myself to be a volunteer

Dreams – what habits and beliefs do I create in order to harness my dreams and aspirations? Firstly, you should know what your goals are. What is your plan for the next year? But for the next five years? Depending on the target, or dream, you must do something daily to get there. Maybe now you are in the development stage, meaning eliminating everything that stops you from getting where you desire as you create new habits and beliefs that will propel you toward your target.

Contribution – What will I do on a daily basis to add more value to the people around me, in order to help? It may be the investment you make in developing some individuals, a financial aid granted to people in need, charitable acts.

After creating a plan for everyone, make sure that you follow it daily, until the values you intend to assimilate and the way in which you're going to do so become part of you, meaning they become habits. Once these values are converted into beliefs and transform into a routine, things will change. Expect to become a more responsible sensitive, intelligent, happy person, or to put it simply, a successful person. Values have the power to lift or drag you down at any time, regardless of your position on the social ladder. Therefore, the last thing you should do is ensure that your values are not reversed. When you are at the point of losing your priorities, you actually lose your organization, which brings with it a chain of negative things, which at some point may destabilize and affect your values.

The problem that most people have today is the order of their priorities. When this is reversed, then both you and your family, and later your company and society will lose. If for example, you make the mistake of putting the desire to earn more above your family then you will find yourself in a position where many people end up. They have succeeded in the domain they wanted, but they ended up miserable, unhappy, and unfulfilled because they've lost the more beautiful and precious thing in the world, namely their family.

Another example, are the people who struggled for years until exhaustion, to earn more money. When they finally succeed, they can no longer enjoy it because their health no longer permits it, and now they have to pay for the money earned with the price of their health. Their life thus becomes a painful journey. Jesus asked, "What's the utility for a man to earn if he'll lose his soul for eternity?" This is the most beautiful statement ever made. Jesus knew this principle: you can have anything you want, but if you don't have health, you will never enjoy your possessions; you can have everything you desire, but if you don't have your family around, all those things become useless.

You must never reverse the priorities because they define the percentage of happiness and success. Success is much more than an Earthly fulfillment. It means to be a fulfilled person, both psychically and especially, spiritually. If your relationship with God is stronger, then your soul (mind, will and emotions) will work very well. When the mind is in excellent shape, then the material prosperity will come because the mind defines how far you'll go and how prosperous you will be. The relationship with family, health, success in life, contribution, all come from the same place called the mind. Therefore, do not forget the order of priorities! The values that you chose as priorities contributes to the life that you live.

1) It determines your value

If you want to truly see what you're worth, then observe the things you harness. You rise only as high as your values. If the values are well established and determined according to their importance and effects they have on people, then your value will become the same. If the values are not clear, but merely assimilated as a result of the environment, or people around you, then your values will be the same. If you truly want to raise your value, then you must set meaningful values, because they represent the base of your value.

It is likely to decrease your value if you waste your time on television, have an unhealthy lifestyle and a defective character. You ask yourself if it's possible for a person to nurture a deficient character or an unhealthy lifestyle. The answer is certainly yes. Anyone who doesn't nurture a healthy lifestyle according to a plan, actually unconsciously does the exact opposite, and anyone who does not harness a strong character, actually nurtures a weak character.

"You can't harness what you don't have!"

155

Your value represents what you are. You will not be able to accomplish a thing which is above you nor give what you don't have. Successful people understood that before giving something valuable, they have to become valuable. Before earning significantly, they must become significant, because they are the factor that determines the gain. You must understand that you are extremely valuable. In fact, you are valued so much that God decided to give you His most treasured son, Jesus. Because God gave everything that was valuable to Him, you became valuable, but in order to own this value you represent, you must do something. Just think of the next illustration: any wood has its importance in the manufacturing process, although it seems to be something very trivial and common. Its importance comes from the thing it is transformed into, from the way in which that product will be used. The wood can be used for fire, in which case, its value is insignificant.

The same wood can be transformed into something different, such as a chair, to be used for different purposes, and its value will increase, being more useful than in the first case. The same piece of wood can be turned into a Stradivarius violin, which is inestimable. Stradivarius violins, built by Antonio Stradivarius are worth millions of dollars being recognized for their impeccable sound that cannot be replicated.

The wood which we've talked about represents you. Many people think that what separates them from those who accomplish significantly. This type of thinking is untrue because their value is also your value. God created us all with the same gift, called potential, which is unlimited. The difference between two people is not defined by what they stand for, but by what he is transformed into. All men are made of the same material, but what makes the difference is the process by which they are transformed.

The reason some people are worth so little is their unwillingness to go through that transformation process. Many of us choose a quick process, or even choose to "burn" ourselves for our own pleasures. Firewood also has its importance but compared with a chair or a Stradivarius violin, it's far too insignificant. The chair, in turn, has value and functionality, but compared to a Stradivarius violin it's far too insignificant. Each of the three examples can contribute something to this world, but the level is always defined by the process through which it passes and the ultimate result obtained. If you choose firewood, you'll be ready in a few minutes to be used; if you choose the chair, then the time will be extended to hours or even days; but if you choose to go through the Stradivarius violin, the days will turn into weeks, weeks into months, until you are ready for functioning. You are the one who must choose in what way you'll transform your life.

God will process you and will only use you at the time you want. If you want your life to be worth more than a few minutes of intense burning, or several years that you are used as a support to assist others, then you have to choose the appropriate process when God will transform you. Don't forget this process will always take a bit more time to prepare. Although you must be processed in detail, the choice will bring you much satisfaction. Your life can become just like a Stradivarius violin, that represents excellence, and from what you become you can touch the hearts of millions or even billions, and your name will remain in history forever. Three things make a difference in a life: process, the thing into which you are transformed and how you will be used.

God can increase the value you have now, more than you have ever imagined if you'll accept being turned into a thing that will influence millions of people. To do this, you need to understand who and what you are now, and what you could become. Do not persist in the idea that you are a simple employee or laborer, that you don't have the needed training, necessary money, that you can't be more than what you are... If you think in this way, I would like to give you good news.

You don't need any of this. The only thing you need is a decision: the decision to let yourself be processed by God. It doesn't matter who you were until now, what counts is what you choose to do with the life you have now. Choose to become everything you can be, through a choice called value. Choose to increase your value in order for your name to be represented by excellence.

2) It determines your life experience

Values determine what you experience in life because it is due to the things you've consciously or unconsciously chosen to fructify. If you choose reading instead of watching television, you'll become a cultivated person, who develops constantly. When you choose to put a value on your family relationships and establish a plan for it, the experiences you extract will be on the same scale, resulting in a healthy, stable, and happy family.

Each one of us chooses what we want to glorify, aware or not, and this choice leads to experimentation.

Increasing value will result in different experiences, therefore, your number one concern must be growth. I told you at the beginning of the book that choices determine actions, resulting in experiences. This is absolutely true! However, take into account changing your experiences by changing the choices and actions determined by the value it represents. You can desire, or even try to choose more wisely than you chose before, with the hope of changing your experiences. Still, the choices change for the better only if your value grows. As long as you stay the same, you'll continue making the same poor choices, that's why it's so vital to keep on growing.

You're probably wondering how you can increase your value. This is possible if you raise the standard of your created values. Define new priorities and emphasize them, such as God, health, reading, relationships, dreams, personal development. All of this will change the life you're currently experiencing into one that you only dream of or didn't even knew existed. People are often frustrated by their experiences, blaming everyone else except themselves.

What they don't realize is that they are the only person who can change something for themselves, but because they deny their responsibilities, they remain with the same frustrations, complaints, and dissatisfaction. I am glad that you are not this kind of person. When you take responsibility and you set your own values, your perception is changed, and the accomplishments you achieve are limitless. No one can determine how far you go, because, with God, all things are possible. Use the value that God has given you, put into practice the values which He demands from you. Then, this life will be the one that God promised. He wants you to live a three- dimensional life.

3) It determines the value you create

The value that you produce is determined by the value you have and comes from the things you fructify. No one can produce a greater value than the one he represents. We raise only at the level of our values. The one who has specified values will have a significant contribution to the world, because of the things he glorifies. When our values are better, we become more valuable and our contribution, and is higher.

You're probably wondering, "Why is the value that you produce so important?" It makes the difference in every area of life. Value makes the difference in your relationships, health, adopted the lifestyle, to the economy and to the money you earn. You can't obtain more hours in a day to earn more money, but you can always become more valuable. The value makes a difference in how much you earn.

The most important lesson in the economy is this: we are paid for the value we produce. Although it takes time to gain this value, you're not paid for time, but for your value. By mistake, we say: "I am paid with this amount of money per hour", but this is not correct because we are not paid for our time, but for the value produced in an hour. The hour is used as a unit of time to assess value.

Is it possible to increase the value and make twice the amount of money at the same time? Or three times, four times? The answer is: of course, you can become more valuable, but only if... There's one if. It is possible to earn several times more in the same number of hours, but only if you offer a higher value. The difference between two people who work in the same domain, the same number of hours, but have different salaries, consists of the value each produces, in the number of hours they work. In order to earn more, you don't need to work more hours, but to put a higher value on the worked hours.

The difference between a sweeper and a doctor does not consist of the worked hours, but the value that each obtains in that period of time. The difference between a simple employee, an engineer, or an economist does not consist in the number of hours, but in the value they put into that number of hours worked. Any value is determined by value. The things you glorify, determine the value you produce.

Chuck Wepner is an example which illustrates well the importance of value. He is famous for the match which he had against the boxing champion Muhammad Ali and who has remained in history. This transformed Chuck into a star. Although nobody gave him a chance, and he was knocked to the ground by the 90th second, before the match finished, losing the match, he became famous because of what happened in the second round. It's all about a punch in the lungs to Ali, knocking him to the ground and causing the public's thrill.

This fight was different from others but was an inspiration for Sylvester Stallone, who was struggling hard at that moment to make a career. Immediately after the match, Stallone went home began writing without interruption, for three days, the screenplay for the well-known movie "Rocky," which was his launch into the film industry. Many producers showed interest in the screenwriting, but Stallone insisted he would sell it only with the condition of playing the first role in the movie.

The bids increased substantially, from a few thousand dollars to over a hundred, the producers wanting an already famous actor in the main role. Although he only had about 100 dollars in his account, Stallone stuck firmly to his position. The bids climbed to $200,000 and even over. Eventually, they agreed that Stallone could play the main role, with the condition that the budget of the film to not go over one million dollars. One of the studios made Chuck Wepner an offer, where he had to choose between accepting 70 thousand dollars just before producing the movie, or a percentage of sales. Because he wanted to play it safe, Wepner chose the seventy-thousand dollar offer, a decision that cost him eight million dollars.

On the same day of March 24, 1975, opportunity passed before both, Sylvester Stallone, as well as Chuck Wepner. Their choices led them to two different destinies and experiences. One ended up a successful actor and writer and continues to enjoy the appreciation of the public and glory, and the other missed the chance, remaining a simple worker. The difference consisted in the value that the two attributed to them.

The same happens when you do not understand the value and the significance you might have in creating a three-dimensional life. Who you are is the most significant wealth you will ever possess. When you understand the importance of own value, you will be able to process it and it will grow, then your life will change. Each day, God offers us a lot of opportunities. By accessing them, our life will transform. You will be surprised to find out that most of us choose like Wepner; we take poor decisions, which subsequently sabotage us.

I wonder how many millions I've lost because of my valueless choices. When we understand who we are and when we realize the value that the Creator gave us, we will put aside the limitations and we'll work on that set of values that truly matter. We will concentrate on them and will form correct priorities, strong faith, great choices, and actions that make all the difference between excellence and mediocrity.

To be certain of positive results, check the values that you set yourself and make sure they suit an excellent lifestyle: moral, prosperous, and happy. Make sure that they resonate with God's principles and ask yourself if you're pleased with them. Will you feel comfortable with sharing them with your friends?

Once set, the values will protect your life from negative influences around you, from wasted time on things that don't matter and from frustrations resulting from less beneficial choices. Understanding and identifying these values will help you become who you desire. Only through understanding and applying them, will you succeed more than you can imagine. You'll manage to do the things that matter and say "no" to things that do not matter. Your productivity and creativity will grow enormously in any field.

All these values are your priorities. They are what you do daily, weekly, monthly and on an annual basis and define what you believe, your beliefs, character, habits, choices, actions, experiences, and the principles that guide your life. They are your DNA, representing the things you struggle for and wish to fructify. They determine your choices and activities, the way you spend and invest. It determines the things you'll accomplish and focus on.

All successful people who achieved something significant in their lives have one thing in common: values they prioritized and followed strictly. You will become a successful person if you take over this truth and create your own values. Values are the principles that guide our lives, determine how far we'll step on the social ladder.

As long as you're alive, you can choose what you do with your life. You can choose to be less than you were meant to be or everything that God created you do be.

a) *The first choice,* is to be less than you're worth, less than your capacity to become great, less than you were created to be; to earn less than you could win; to have less than you could have; to try less than you could try; to read and think less than you could ; to live less than you could; to dream less than you could dream; to believe less than you could; to be less happier than you could; to help and love less than you could. These are choices which lead to an empty and unfulfilled life. The good news is that you can change these choices because there are better ones.

b) *The second choice,* is to be everything you could be; to become everything you can; to read every book you can read in order to develop; to earn as much as you can, to give as much as you can; to believe, to dream of becoming great and influential; to become stronger, more loving, understanding; to become a successful person who makes a difference in the world, to live a three-dimensional life.

The choice is yours: to be or not to be, to become or not to become, to do or not to do. You can become the person that God created. The choice belongs to you. Why not do everything that stands in your power, in the best way you can and for as longer as you can? God created you to do something significant in this world, not only to pass through it. Do not let yourself be limited by less than your value. Keep in mind that the reward is reserved for those who add value to people and the world, as a result of their dream of becoming someone.

13

Principles

Just as there are universal laws that govern nature, so there are principles that govern our lives. Once understood and applied, they influence the course of our lives in every moment, with every choice we make. These principles apply to each person, regardless of culture, religion, age, education, or social position. Principles describe how someone uses everything, in order to form a style of life. Principles give life a direction. A principle is a strong belief that you made about a particular thing. The quality of our principles will determine the quality of the experience, and quality of experiences determine the quality of life. To create a principle means to be an intuitive person, meaning to prepare for a big surprise, to know how to enjoy the day it will come.

If you have a conviction or a principle about how you relate to things that life brings to you, then the choices will always be profitable and beneficial. When you decide what you will do in a certain situation, even if you don't experience it now, you will have an opportunity to relate to it correctly.

Let's assume that you've decided to create a life principle with regards to the emotional status. You have now determined that, no matter what situation you experience, you will keep your calm and optimism, so you will be able to choose consciously, without being influenced, and see the positive side and take advantage of it.

By setting goals for yourself and creating a belief in this direction, you can to be one hundred percent sure that, when a conflict or bad news emerges, you will remain calm and positive, even though it will be painful.

Maybe you wonder how it is possible, or if it is possible? It sounds very good, but is it really so simple? The fact is that it is one hundred percent possible. When a belief has been created, then the information resulting from the experiences will be taken up by the brain, but before the consciousness decides, it will pass through the subconscious, where it is checked by the filter called beliefs. If the information is bad, hard or negative, the subconscious will stop it right there and reject it, remembering that you must stay calm, positive and ask yourself what you might learn from that situation.

Sounds so nice, huh? Well, this is the truth that you must understand in order to take advantage of the wonderful complexities that God has put in you. The reality is that each of us already has a principle for the emotional state from our subconscious, which can be positive or negative, depending on what you allowed to form inside. If when your emotional state is provoked, you burst and become violent, depressed, or negative, then it is clear that over time, you've taught your subconscious mind that this is your way of reacting, and now it guides you. If you feel like saying a few unkind words to someone who doesn't please you, then again, the subconscious reacts as it was taught. It knows you feel good when saying a few nasty words, because after all, you're important. Others must fear you, and you get satisfaction and fulfillment from this.

What you must understand is simple: we will experience effectively those principles that we form in the subconscious. If they are good, positive, and beneficial, then you will live a fulfilled and beautiful life, because the risks of adopting a wrong attitude in any situation are reduced. Instead, if you have never created principles in a conscious way, but you left everything to chance and they've formed 'all by themselves', depending on events, you will experience problems that will lead to consequences. In order to be sure of obtaining positive results under any circumstances, you must ensure that you have very good principles about everything in life. You need to create principles about your character and its components.

For example, Integrity-regardless of the circumstances.

I will choose the truth and only the truth. I won't accept compromises, not even for a moment. What I will say, I will do and what I'll do, I'll say. My "Yes" will be "Yes", and my "No" will be "no ". If you are going to create such a principle about integrity, it will be easy when opportunities or thoughts come and urge you to choose otherwise. Your belief will warn you about what is not good. However, if you don't have such a principle, you will wake up in front of opportunities to deceive or choose something other than integrity and you'll compromise yourself. Thus, you will suffer greatly, both you and the company, Church, family, or partner. In other words, your environment is influenced by the choices you make.

Ten principles of life

1) Principle for thoughts

I redirect my thoughts, not the other way around. I accept the thoughts that I allow or repel. I will use a filter for the thoughts that try to transform into beliefs. I will not allow negative thoughts to influence my state of mind and emotions. The only one that will have room in my mind is the Holy Spirit. I do not accept thoughts of fear, concern, immoral and negative. Such a principle will always direct you positively. To have a principle for your thoughts means to coordinate your life because of thought channels and determine every experience.

What is your principle for thoughts? You choose depending on your thoughts, or depending on the filter through which you have checked them? If you don't know how to give truthful answers, it means you do not have a filter, so you'll need to form it. Decide how you will be influenced by your everyday thoughts. Tell yourself how you want to relate to them when they come. Create a principle and your thoughts will be positively directed.

2) Principle for beliefs

To create a principle means to create a belief. Beliefs will influence a great number of your choices, that's why you need to decide right now how you'll form a belief. Tell yourself: "From now on, my principle is the following: I will not let anybody influence the forming of my beliefs. Only after I verify the information I receive about a thing, will I decide what definition to give it. I will not allow the formation of any negative belief. Based on my filter, I'll check the formation of my future beliefs".

3) Principle for my choices
My choices will always be based on thoughts and checked beliefs. I will not take any important decision without checking the filter which reveals the best choice. I will always check if that belief doesn't come into contradiction with my character, beliefs, thoughts and God's morality.

4) Principle for actions
Actions are summaries of the choices we've taken consciously or unconsciously. Will my actions be well-thought out, resulting from great choices? I will not act in a stressed emotional state. I will not be led by temporary impulses or emotional states of mind, but I'll think of the consequences.

5) Principle for a relationship
Form a principle about what the relationships you enter look like. What kind of person do you want to choose as your life partner? In what kind of circle of friends will you immerse yourself? What kind of relationship do you have with God? The principle of relationships is as follows: the relationships in which I enter must be positive relations, from which I can learn, be challenged and grow. The relationships that I form won't affect the values I have.

6) Principle for the character
The principle of the character determines what kind of character you'll have. Maybe today you are proud of your character. Everyone appreciates you for it. However, it is not enough because, at some point, your character will be challenged. In that moment, if there isn't a strong belief that

validates the character, you'll fall and you'll lose the qualities that you enjoy today. A principle for the character means to assimilate assets and ascribe it to this principle. No matter what happens around me, I will remain an honest person; what I'll say, that's what I'll do; I'll be responsible, in every situation I will assume responsibility; I'll be patient; I will persevere and I will use my time, no matter how long or short it may be, to achieve what I want; I will relate to the things around with a correct attitude; I'll be flexible and remain open to change and growth; I'll have the courage to face any situation. Create such a principle and your character will remain strong, regardless of the challenges.

7) Principle for problem

Nothing and nobody will be able to stop me from what I want to accomplish. I will use problems to help me grow. I will learn from every problem and difficulty what God has intended for me. Problems are not meant to lead towards my destruction, but for my growth. Henry Ford said, "Failure is the opportunity to try again, but more wisely. The principle of the problem is that there are no problems. For me, problems are opportunities".

8) Principle for health

Many people live being unconscious of the importance of health until they get to experience a loss or a suffering in the body. Only then, do they wake up to reality. To have a principle for health is vital for each person because every achievement in life depends on health. A healthy person is more creative, stronger, agile, capable and more beautiful. When people create their own principles for health, they become happier, more fulfilled, satisfied because they have more confidence in them.

Do you have a principle for health? Most people go through life being unconscious of the importance of health until they face the shattering reality. Without this sort of general rule, you risk failing. Imagine a person who grew up in a poor family, with low financial possibilities, but who became prosperous. The first thing that scientists identified in these situations is gaining weight. Of course, along with gaining weight, come other issues, such as the change in the physical appearance, suffering metabolism, and increased cholesterol. All of them come as a package, because now, a person can eat everything he wants from a large variety of things. No matter if you're poor or rich, what you must do to have very good health is to create a principle.

Health is on the list of my priorities. I will not allow myself to lose my health, because I would lose my ability to continue helping people, to be creative and to grow. My principle for health is the following: three days a week I do sports, I consume healthy food and sleep seven or at most, eight hours a night. Following this principle, I grew a lot physically, psychically, and spiritually. Now, although there are days when I feel like eating or to drinking something other than healthy things, my subconscious stops and tells me: "No, no, no, you are not allowed to eat that cookie, or to drink that beverage because it's not good for your health!" In this way, I reject them and go on. Of course, there are days when I make exceptions and eat less healthily. However, on these days, the subconscious is telling me that I am not allowed. I tell it that today is the day when I make an exception and then the subconscious is retiring and I can eat in peace, without feeling guilty.

Create your own principle for health. It doesn't have to be the same as mine. Create a unique one, but do not forget that it'll determine how you experience health in the future.

9) Principle for time

Time is very important for everyone. We're all limited by time, depending on what we choose to do with it. People complain often about the constant passing of time: "There is so much to do and so little time!" I don't believe in this theory and I am not a fan of it. I believe that successful people will always find time for success, in the same way that careless people find a way to lose it.

The principle concerning time determines the way you will manage it. If you've didn't intentionally form it and if you don't have discipline in your subconscious, then you're following a harmful and negative principle. I know exactly how I manage my time. It does not manage me, but I manage it. Each day, I have enough time to do the things I consider important. You'll find time if you set a clear principle to apply in mind.

Mediocre people waste their time depending on what the day brings, but successful people know precisely how to use their time, each day. They know the things they must do and act in this direction. What are the most important things that you must do daily? Write them down somewhere and establish a principle for a period of time. In this way, you will always have enough time for them.

10) Principle for growth

Growth is primarily made up of the necessity to grow progressively. No matter how much I know, there are still things that I should find out and haven't yet, books I should read which I haven't read, people I should meet and haven't met, places I ought to visit and haven't visited, people I should help and haven't.

The growth principle consists of two components:

a) Gathering information

- Notes – means to always have with you an instrument for writing. Many believe that they don't need notes, but it is not wise to have such a mindset because the things you hear and don't write get lost within 48 hours.
- Observation – means that whoever you are meeting or any place that you visit, you will notice three or five new things. When you wake up in the morning, propose the following objective: today I want to notice three new things, that I've not noticed until now, meaning I will learn something from this day. Having such an attitude, you schedule your brain to observe what you want. Then you will very easily find the things which will contribute enormously to your growth. The secret is to adopt the right attitude, and the rest will

come by itself, that's why attitude is an important component of the character.

b) Applying information

- Means to apply everything you've learned in your life. See where the things we've noted and observed fit well and apply them. The application makes the difference, but for sure, you have nothing to apply until you learn.

All of the ten principles listed above are laws that govern and influence our life directly or indirectly, according to conjuncture. If we don't become aware of them and their implementation in our personal life, we'll wake up at some point being overwhelmed, without knowing what to choose. Then, the chances of making wrong choices are very high. It is totally different when you wake up in front of challenges, and in your subconscious, you have a clear principle, because you know exactly what you are going to choose, without feeling pressured and surpassed. If, for example, you are convinced that smoking is terrible and harmful to the health, you know you should stay away from it, then you know what happens when you face the opportunity to smoke. Even if you are offered a sum of money along with the proposal to smoke, would you reject the proposal? Why? Because you have a principle with regard to tobacco, according to which you make your choices.

The good news is that all people have principles. The bad news is that most of them were unconscious, formed according to experiences, images sent to the brain, what they've felt and how it was perceived by those senses. The reason you will always find extremely talented people on one side is that their principles are not good. Each person is either good or bad, according to his principles. For example, we call people with character, those who have three or four components of character, which emphasize their positive parts, although they have others that reveal their negative parts. However, because the good ones outweigh the bad, she is a good person. The same is true of the person who has more bad than good principles. The bad part is more visible, and we say that this is a man without character. The reality is that all of these people are potential people with character if their principles change. But because most are unaware of what causes them to choose in this manner, they remain the same.

Regardless of which category you belong to, what you need to know is that you're a wonderful person, created by God to accomplish great things. Talent, ability, and potential that God has put in you must be freed, but before you must set aside all the things that limit us, and these are the wrong beliefs.

So far, I think you've discovered every negative belief that pulled you down and changed it. If not, then please go back to the chapter on beliefs and check them, using the given pattern, and then, after you've identified them, change them. If you did this, I wish to lead you to the final step needed in order to enjoy the maximum results. This is the formation of the principles that govern your life positively and beneficially. Perhaps you are an exemplary person but have noticed a small rupture in your character. I urge you to solve that crack, for better results. Maybe you're a person who has many cracks; then you need to fix each one of them. No matter who or what you are, you have the right to live beautifully and blessed, that's why you are on this Earth.

If there are areas in your life where you do not know how to choose and act, because you have not formed principles for them, then all you have to do is to visualize them.

Imagine that you find yourself in the midst of a circumstance for which you want to create a principle. Observe your reaction towards that circumstance; what will you do? If you don't know what to reply, it means that you do not have a set principle and you need to work on this.

For example, I've made up a principle about any news that I receive. My principle is the following: when I receive horrible news, I'll keep calm, I will remain positive and I will address myself questions such as: what does God want me to learn? How can I use this terrible news? Is there something good in it? How could I fix it? How can I use it for my own good? From the moment I laid down this principle and until today, I've never been disappointed, depressed, or worried, upon receiving negative news. Even if negative thoughts have tried to come, my belief stopped them, and I was able to ask the suitable questions and, indeed, I have always found something good in news that first appeared to be bad.

Maybe you're thinking that it sounds great, but how can such a principle solve your problem? The answer is that it will solve the problem. The question that I need to ask is not if problems will come, but when they come, because problems come irrespective of who you are; the difference is how you will respond to them. Problems are not problems for me because I choose not to believe in them, that's why, when I am in such moments, I remember that I'm in front of opportunities. Over time, each of them proved to be disguised opportunities. So, what will I do to resolve them? Once a principle is rooted, you will know how to solve them. This means that once problems come, you have the solution and you will not forever live in fear but with the hope that they will not come anymore.

When problems arise, the principles will help you turn them into opportunities. If you do not have principles for problems, then they will become problems, and for some this will be the reason for quitting, which leads to failure. Never will God give us things that we can't resolve, but we tend to complicate and transform them into a true tragedy because we don't know how to respond to them.

A person who has no principles after which he guides his life ends up prey for the circumstances. Principles are designed to protect us from challenging and difficult moments, but at the same time, to lead us toward an accomplished life. God left principles written in the Bible, and when we follow them, we become prosperous, happy, and fulfilled.

14

How to Choose

When I was little, my parents used to constantly tell me that the choices I make in life would affect my actions and then my experiences. "Be careful how you choose!" they said to me, "because life goes just one way. Once you have chosen a path, you can no longer go back into the past and change the choice you've made, that's why every decision has its own consequence. When you make a choice, you choose the experience that will result from it."

Being aware of choice's importance, I went to school, where again I was told that truth. Becoming an adult, I've had to deal with my own decisions, in which parents and teachers were no longer involved. Growing up in a Christian church, I heard repeatedly how important my future choices are. But though I was constantly told how important choices are, too few told me how to choose very well. I knew that it was important to choose wisely, but I didn't know how to do it.

Maybe you are struggling with such a situation, that's why I decided to help you make these choices. The examples I give you will produce extraordinary results.

Myself and many others who listened to this example experienced not just financial, physical, and psychological growth, but more than that: happiness and fulfillment at a higher level. Imagine how your life would look, if you'd chosen differently in a specific situation. Do you feel that there are so many things that, if you'd chosen differently, would have led you to a much better result? There are so many opportunities to choose.

Unfortunately, you can't go back to the past and change anything in your present, as a result of the choices you've made. What you can do, but you must start from this point on, is to choose differently, in order for your future to look different and so you can experience an extraordinary life, resulting from extraordinary choices. From now on, when you are faced with a difficult choice, you'll want to check it before you decide how to choose.

You are struggling with a difficult choice that you're not sure of and you don't know what to do? Thoughts are extremely important because they determine our beliefs, which in turn, establish our choices, which determine our actions, which, in the end, determine results and experiences. The choices are extremely importance, as well as the beliefs and thoughts that we allow into our minds. However, there are moments in life when choices are difficult. It can be about a choice which is not influenced by any belief. It may be positive and negative thoughts that torment you. As such you don't know what is best to choose. You may choose in one way, but there are certain risks. You choose in another way, but again there are risks.

The question is how to choose in such situations. These are the most important choices you need to take because they exceed you, your beliefs, and capacity. In such a situation, everything depends on the thoughts that cross your mind. In order to choose well in such situations, you need to check your thoughts and the risks implied by each choice. Before checking the choice through the filter of the four steps, I suggest you do the most important thing: pray and ask God to enlighten you, so you can choose being guided by the Holy Spirit and thus, to take the best decision.

Five steps you need to follow if you want to choose wisely

1) Identifying – What kind of thoughts do I have, positive or negative?

What do I feel inside about this decision I want to make? Do I feel fear, concern, uncertainty, or the opposite? Do I feel that it's a choice that reinforces my spirit, which motivates me? You're not sure what to choose, however, you can discover what kind of thoughts nurture that choice. If the thoughts are negative, it is possible that the choice may also have negative effects. For example, if it creates concern, fright, blurriness, uncertainty, then you have to put to question it.

2) Origin – Where do these thoughts come from? Are these from God or from the devil? Identify them and you'll discover their origin. Pay attention to the details! If the choice involves breaking morality, it doesn't come from God. Every thought we have influences our decisions, either positively, or negatively. The Bible states that the Holy Spirit is the one that guides us in every choice we make, therefore, if you want to choose well, make sure that the guide behind your choice is the Holy Spirit. He always puts reality in front of us, to help us choose correctly. However, the decision belongs to us; whether we accept the devil's manipulation towards a wrongful and damaging path or the Holy Spirit's guidance.

Ask yourself: do you have to lie, steal, and cheat in that situation? Then you know for sure that it is not a good choice. However, there will be times that they will have nothing to do with morality, therefore, in such moments you must refer your choice to the third point.

3) Need – After identifying the choice over which you want to decide and discovering its source, and if it breaks God's morality or not, the third step comes when you need to check the need for the choice in question. Ask yourself if you need it. There is a significant difference between wanting a thing and needing it. Wanting means wishing, but needing means necessity. Very often we choose wrongly, driven by desires and not necessities.

Example: "I need a car to ease my work" - this is a necessity. "I want the latest car model on the market, or a top brand, in order to impress and show off who I am" - this is a wish. Of these two, it is wise to buy the car you can afford that meets your needs, and not the one which helps you impress others and for which you do not have the necessary resources. You can't go into debt to satisfy a wish. Always, priorities consist of needs, not desires. Desires are very good, but only when wisely used.

Another example might be: "I must eat healthily to maintain my healthy body", compared to "I want to eat everything I desire". In this case, what you want to do is to eat according to your body's needs, rather than eating what you know is unhealthy. The wise choice is keeping a balance, for the maintenance of physical and mental health. If you want to go to a specific place, but the need pushes you to go elsewhere, then the wise decision is to follow the order of your priorities and first to go wherever it is needed.

Before taking a decision, consider if it is mandatory to do it, to go to that place, or to buy the object in question. The order of the priorities is the need, then come the desires. Successful people choose in order of their priorities. The one who chooses wisely, in accordance with the need he has, usually gets to experience the fulfillment of his dreams. But the one who chooses to be led by desires, not only remains unfulfilled once his desire is fulfilled, but has to suffer due to unresolved needs.

Very often in life, it is simple to choose, if we see the difference between the two, the need and desire. The desire, once satisfied, passes, but the need continues for a long time and you cannot progress if you don't solve it. Analyze your thoughts and conclude if it's a need or a wish.

4) Result – Before making a decision, you should take into consideration the possible results; the benefits and risks. If you're in a leadership function, be careful of the choices you make and the risks for the people you lead over. If you're in a business, pay attention to the risks to which you submit your business. If you are a husband, be aware of the risks you submit your wife, through financial, emotional, and physical choices.

Let's assume that behind these decisions you have good and positive thoughts. This is an important step because you've gracefully passed by the first two stages. You know you'll choose in this manner, but now you don't want to choose before verifying how to do so. You can't only take into account the positive and negative side, but also the potential profit or loss, resulting from your choice. If you can't approximate your risks, possible losses, or gains, then try talking with others who have chosen similarly.

For any decision that you will ever take, there will be people from which you could learn and have experienced the results of similar choices. Learn from them. Check to see what they've experienced following the election. How is their life as a result? How are they following the decision taken? The questions will bring you clarification. Perhaps the result was hurtful to them, which means that the chances of the same are high for you. As an example, consider an offer made to you, with the promise of a huge winning. The offer is very good, but there is a problem.

In order to benefit from it, you are asked certain things that break your values and principles, namely your integrity and morality. What will you choose? If you accept, it means stepping over your dignity as a person, although the win would provide a nice living for a long time. If you refuse, it means keeping your dignity but losing out. These choices are the most difficult ones; that's the reason many choose incorrectly.

The blur of such choices is engendered by our thoughts because the interpretation is wrong. It is not the choice which makes the decision difficult, but the way in which we perceive it. A choice that requires breaking some principles and values is never advisable, being more an indicator of degradation and failure. If you fix this clearly in your mind, you'll understand that a choice which requires lying, for example, ruins you. Sooner or later, this lie will require another one to cover it and, at some point, you'll be a servant to this lifestyle.

A wise person always learns from other people's experiences. Propose to yourself to be among those wise people, who, prior to choosing, check the results experienced by others. Maybe it won't be the case that you'll break morality, however, by a simple verification, you will be able to make a plan that will save you both time and the costs of the choice in question. Don't forget that through the choice you make, you also choose the outcome.

Answering to these four questions, you will be able to observe if their nature is positive or negative. At the same time, you'll see the gains or losses resulting from one choice or another. Questions are like an alarm clock that wakes you up to reality: ourselves. How many times have you been disappointed by a good choice you've made? Never, huh? A good choice always brings benefits and then the only disappointment is that you didn't do it faster. If today you become aware of the importance of a great choice, then in the future, you will experience very good results. Analyzing the questions, not only will you decrease the chances of an unwise choice, but you'll consistently increase the chance of a wise and beneficial choice. Making good decisions is very important at every moment, because a decision influences the next, and so on.

Example: If you wrongly choose a financial investment and produce a loss, in the future, every financial decision will be influenced by the first, because that loss restricts and affects the way you manage money. Now, you're limited by the decision taken. Starting from today, you will invest time and attention in the choices you make, so in the future, you'll collect the results of your choice. Maybe you imagine that you need a lot of time to make such a decision, or you may feel surpassed by so many details that you need to take them into account.

No matter what you think, one thing you need to be aware of; it is wiser to invest more time in making a very good decision than to change a wrong decision. Forming the habit of choosing well, at some point, will become a belief, a principle, which in time will become automatic. We choose daily, consciously or unconsciously. We decide, but whatever we decide; that will be our experience. Start to check the choice you have to make right now and you'll see how easy and beneficial this criterion is.

How to choose when I'm insecure, even if I've used the filter?

There are exceptions in which, no matter how hard you try to decide, it is impossible to do it. These are normal times and usually take place when someone is so emotionally and physically involved in that choice, that they can't perceive logic. Thus, emotions and emotional involvement make the choice difficult.

Isn't it true that you know people who should change and you wonder how they didn't see the thing that pulls them down, making them choose wrongly? It is so visible to you because you're not sentimentally and emotionally involved. The same happens sometimes with us, because of the involvement. So, instead of seeing reality, we see an illusion which makes us see that particular thing or choice as being best, when, frankly, we are far from the truth. In such case cases, advice is all that we need.

Although these moments are rare, they are usually the most important ones, because they concern things that exceed ourselves. They are, if you will, the choices that make the difference. The question is how do I decide what to choose in such situations? Well, after you've tried and ensured that it is impossible for you to draw a conclusion, you need to enable what I call, discerning. It is simple and consists of asking for the opinion and aid from various people around you. Search for the people in whom you can trust, explain your situation, and ask them, what would they choose if they were in your place? These people can be your lover, partner, leader, pastor, mentor, friend, parents, relatives, colleagues, or anyone else you trust. By asking questions, you will be able to discover other useful opinions. However, my suggestion is to find not only people who have an opinion, but rather, people who have been through the same or similar situations and who chose well, and as a result had good results.

Therefore, you must do three things:

1) *Identify* – Firstly, identify the area in which you are struggling, with the choice you're not sure of. What should you choose and don't know how to? Identification is very simple, so, once you know what it's about, you move to the next step.

2) *Search for a competent person* – Find the right person who can give you a good suggestion and has experience in what you currently experience. If you do not find anybody who has been through a similar situation, seek a virtual friend (internet) and analyze. Or, just ask those around you, even if they haven't gone through what you have. Maybe they can give you a suggestion. Each suggestion counts. However, search for the right person

and place, or in other words, don't go to the doctor to fix a car and don't go to the mechanic to fix back pain.

3) Decides – Gather the information and suggestions that you've received and review them through the filter which I gave you, to see if they are beneficial or not. Once you have discovered the risks and possible effects, you can decide how to choose.

Believe it or not, the reality we experience is due to thoughts, so, if you're going to take this seriously, I believe from the bottom of my heart that your life will change. Not because it's a good motivation or because it sounds good, but because I have seen countless times, with my own eyes, people who experienced a major change in their lives due to this checking model.

Now, after you have changed or will change every habit and negative belief that you had or have, you must use this filter for the rest of your life, through which you can check the thoughts that go through your mind daily. In any form, you must not allow the thoughts coming from the devil to make a nest in your mind and heart. It is very good that you eliminated the beliefs which limited you or habits and addictions that pulled you down, but it is not enough.

I want you to keep going; to feed yourself with positive, constructive, encouraging thoughts, coming from God, and not with useless and harmful thoughts. You have to understand that at any time you can change a belief if you allow only a certain kind of thought to make a nest. Protect your life through the protection and selection of thoughts. Keep this book and it read it all over again whenever you're struggling with difficult choices or uncontrollable thoughts and you will find the solution again. The life that God gave us is too short to throw away and too long to waste.

The circumstances and problems of life don't form us but reveal who we are. Therefore, don't wait for problems to occur in order to find out who you are, but form yourself, so that you control the problems.

A person who has principles, values and beliefs about everything in life will know how to relate to them, but the one person who doesn't have principles will go along with the wave, in the direction of the flow. You are the one who controls the direction of your boat's flow, but in order to control it, you must know where you're heading. In other words, where do you want to go?

How do I react to other people's choices?

1) When I relate to someone else's choices, that have affected me, I can choose to respond and provoke an argument, or I may not respond, but deep inside to be affected by that choice. The result, in this case, will be thoughts or even negative beliefs about that person and a gradual rupture of the bond we had. It is possible to control my thoughts and not respond, by not wanting to help the one who is wrong, to help him change. This situation works, if the man is not part of my circle and it's just a foreign person. If, however, it happens to be a close friend, then it is very likely that he may repeat the mistake and I'll be affected again. In such a circumstance, is wise to help him.

2) I can choose not to respond, to provoke an argument, but in the meantime, not to be affected inside by those negative thoughts caused by the other's choice. In this situation, I have one option, namely to make that person aware of the responsibility that he has and the negative effect produced by the respective choice, but also, on the whole group, whether that is in an institution, Church, business, community, group, the circle of friends.

Pay attention when trying to make the person in question responsible for his mistake! Most target the mistake, which is inefficient. Odd! Then I wonder, how am I supposed to act with maximum efficiency? The answer is by presenting the positive side. Don't tell him what mistakes he made, but tell him how well he manages, what qualities he has and only then introduce the mistake in the form of a character crack. For example, if I am employed and want to make my boss aware of his repeated mistakes that affect both him and us, I must start with the positive side: how well the business goes, how well he manages it, how profitable the earnings, and so on. Afterward, I will introduce the mistake, telling him: "I think that you could do better! For a better profit, for a better functioning, for efficient growth, you might consider a different choice in this area. You have a much too good business to make this kind of mistake". With such a presentation I have the chance to be able to convince him to change his choices, which of course, will affect me later.

The same goes for marriage, career, friends, family, etc. Such an approach brings maximum results. However, if the first attempt doesn't work, continue to persevere. You must remember that mistakes that come from belief are implemented strongly in the brain, therefore, for achieving results, the opposite must be repeated until the belief changes. The result will come in time, even if at first, is doesn't work. The bonus you will receive in the end will consist of the wonderful relationship you build and your successful career. All of this due to the character you cultivate today.

At one point, my wife went through a similar experience. Being at a training school for four months, she met all sorts of people more or less responsible, and the problem was their choices. Often, when I talked with her, she was frustrated and dissatisfied with other's choices. I remember how she presented the wrong choices of those around and that affected her. At some point, she got ill from the negligence of some people who had the virus. Her frustration came from the fact that for a whole week she had to suffer because of the negligence of those around her. But after she regained her health, her frustrations continued because of the people in question, that is, her fellow colleagues, continued to make the same wrong choices.

One day, not long after she regained her health, she woke up with a headache. She claimed that it was due to her room-mate, who coughed and sneezed everywhere, spreading germs, without covering her mouth. Talking with her, she had two choices, to do exactly as I wrote above: either overcome the situation, replacing the negative thoughts and continue to be frustrated throughout her stay there, or to speak with her colleague and make her aware of her mistakes.

Understanding the importance of a discussion, she chose to speak with her, but as a result of the conversation, she was deeply marked by the difficulties encountered. During this time, she had accused a person undergoing an ordeal that no one knew anything about. Understanding her problems, my wife apologized and changed her attitude, and if until that moment she viewed her colleague as uneducated, now she began helping her. All she had to do was to modify her beliefs towards the person in question and help her understand that some things need to be done differently. From that point on, they became best friends. My wife enjoyed the company and discipline of her roommate, and the colleague found a true friend, who was by her side.

I've shared this story because you, just as my wife can find yourself in similar situations. Do not forget one thing: you never know what a person goes through, the one you accuse in your subconscious. No man is bad inside, but beliefs, thoughts, and negative habits make him choose wrongly. Help the person that you now hate to overcome his problems. Be a friend, not a judge, the boss, partner, friend, uncle, cousin, or maybe even the neighbor are in need of someone who may have enough courage to get over their shallowness and help them. Even if they seem strong on the outside, don't forget that the battles are inside. Failures and victories are determined from the inside. Pride and arrogance are only the weaknesses through which they attempt to hide their battles. That dull seriousness they pose is nothing but a desperate cry for help. You, instead, choose to help people change and this will change not only their lives but also your life, because their choices will affect you, in a certain proportion.

15

One Thing You Can't Choose

In life, you can choose everything. God gave you the gift of choice, through which you can relate to everything, regardless of its nature. You can choose almost anything, from small things like eating or dressing, to the most meaningful, like how you relate to God, to people, to yourself, to society, to the values you choose to follow, to your thoughts, images you give these thoughts, your beliefs, choices, actions, feelings you create, things you focus on and many other things.

You can choose everything in life, except from one: the consequence of what you choose. It always comes as a result of your choices. Just think of a simple choice you had, like what to eat. Every day, you had the possibility to pick out what you want to eat, like healthy food or junk food, but now you have to deal with it. Your body will be just like you wanted, just as healthy, fit, and beautiful as you like. Nobody wants to have this type of consequence, but only the one that results from your decision. If you don't like the consequence you experience, change the choices, but you cannot choose is the consequence of your actions. If you realize that, you'll truly understand why you've experienced what you did and of course, its effects, both negative and positive, which resulted from your choices.

Do you want different consequences? Change your choices. Growing up in the Church since I was little, I learned that Jesus came into the world to die for me and for you and give us the opportunity to be saved. Saved from what? I never really understood why, until I realized this truth. Why did Jesus have to come to Earth in order to die? Wouldn't it have been easier just to accept everyone in Heaven, no matter what? After all, we are His creation and He loves us all the same. Jesus had to come to this world due to this reality, called "the consequence". He couldn't change our choices because of His correct judgment. It meant that He would trespass His own justice. However, He did one thing: He sent Jesus to the world in order to positively influence us and proclaim the truth. Those who heard Him, in turn, were to influence others, and so on, so that we all have the possibility to change our destination, and also the choices we make in this process and the consequences that arise. Jesus had to die because He had to pay the price of the sin and through this price, we were given a second chance. His purpose was not just to die for our sins. Of course, this gave us a second chance but if your choices are still the same, then the consequence is death. Before He granted His forgiveness, Jesus wanted to influence our lives through the truth that he embodies. By means of the truth, we had to change our options as well as the outcome.

In conclusion, what was His purpose? It had two different parts: the first one was to come to the world and influence people in a positive way, to help them choose positively. The second purpose was to die for the people and as a result of this, the price of the sin to be paid so we can have the possibility of starting from scratch, renewed and forgiven for all our sins that we should have paid for with death. Through Jesus's death, this price was paid and we received a new life, which means a new chance. Today, you and I have to choose if we accept and take advantage of this chance, changing our choices, and of course, our consequences. You and I have our lives ahead of us to choose what and how we want to live our second chance, but eventually, we will die someday.

Our life will be mirrored in our death. If you chose well, you will experience a good consequence, beyond death, but if you didn't take the chance, this you will experience a bad consequence beyond death. The choice you've made in life will determine your consequence in death.

Check what I said and don't let your beliefs and choices be influenced negatively and I promise you will find happiness. No matter how hard we've tried to find an excuse for our choices, consequences will still be there. Right? Even if we chose unintentionally, thoughtlessly, and involuntarily, the consequences still remain. In everything in life, you'll have the possibility to choose, that's why I strongly advise you to choose wisely, in order to have an extraordinary life. But be aware of the other one as well, because in the end, there will be a conclusion for each choice, and that will be the consequence that cannot be changed.

Jesus came to influence us in a good way and give us the possibility of a new life. It's up to you how you act. God never wanted us to suffer, nor sent anyone to Hell. These things are the consequences of the life we chose to live. God did everything he could for us humans, from the beginning to Jesus, and from Jesus to the Holy Spirit, who is with and in us, and through His Word, the Bible, it constantly motivates us to choose positively, to choose life. "Life is like a dime; you can spend it on whatever you want, but only once." God gave you everything you need to become a successful person. Don't limit yourself by doing little things, because you were created to do great things. The world we live in needs people with strong character, influential, moral, in every area of the society to convert into God's plan. A quote from the Bible says: "Here, I put in front of you good and evil; Choose the good." Choose a three-dimensional life. Not only a wealthy one, but also a spiritual one. To live a life of success means living a continuous success for the rest of life. A wise man said: "never pay the price for an investment". You enjoy the result of an investment but you also pay the price for not investing.

You do not pay a price for the investment that you make in a life of success, however, you enjoy all the benefits you experience as a result of such a life. You pay the price of limitations, unhappiness, insecurity, frustrations, addictions, depression, negative habits and much more. You do not pay a price for a relationship in which you invest, but enjoy every benefit that you extract from this relationship, such as happiness, satisfaction, love and safety, confidence, affection, but you surely pay a price for not investing in it. You do not pay a price for choosing to become a child of God. By contrast, you benefit from this choice by being a child of God, such as living an ethical life, having health, prosperity, happiness, fulfillment, satisfaction, confidence, faith, hope, and love, more than all this, eternal life. However, there is a price that you pay if you do not become a child of God. It is the price of a wasted, unhappy life in which you are unfulfilled and without respect, full of insecurity and worries. Being a child of God means to enjoy all the benefits of this withdrawal, but not being his child means to pay the price.

Many of us live embraced by all sorts of fears which have no role other than to keep us away from our dreams. Some fear death and Hell when in fact, they should fear to live their life irresponsibly, wasting it. Hell is nothing but the result of choosing to live this life being guided by your pleasure. Others fear failure when in fact, they should fear the lack of personal development, because failure is nothing else but the poor result of our choices. Choose to take advantage of all the benefits of a successful life, by choosing to live a life with God. The price of a life wasted is too high, therefore do not forget one thing: you will never pay a price for the things in which you invest, but you will always pay a price for things that you do not invest in. Choose to invest in this life you have. Use this book as a guide, to direct your life choices and to obtain consequences of joy.

The Bible presents the most accurate picture of what it means to choose life. In the Old Testament is presented an image in which Moses, as a leader over Israel named by God, asks the people to choose between life and death. What did they choose? Logically speaking, they ought to choose life because nobody wishes to die, especially if he has the opportunity to choose. Unfortunately, except for two men, their choice was death. Are you wondering, how can anybody choose so badly? Well, the question didn't refer to the earthly life or death, it had to do with the way they choose to live further.

Moses' question is the question that I want to address you at the end of this book. Knowing you have just one life, what will you choose? Live an ethical life? Develop your best self? Do you choose to live a happy, moral, prosperous, and successful life? Or choose to live disappointed, frustrated, dissatisfied, and unhappy? Israel has chosen in those times to continue living their irresponsible lives, tortured in the wilderness. Two of them, however, Caleb and Joshua, chose life. Following their choice, they became heroes who will remain in history forever, due to their achievements. What do you choose?

Choose Life and you will live!
Choose a 3D life!

Dear reader,

Congratulations on your investment through which you contributed to your growth. Congratulations for everything you've learned and congratulations on everything you will apply in your life. I want to believe, along with you, that your life will never be the same. I think that you made a decision that will bring you different experiences. Now, you have come to the end of this book, but still, at the beginning of a 3D life. My encouragement to you is act! The first step will make the difference. Take everything you've learned and apply it to your life, and if you know someone who might benefit from this book, if you think that you were blessed to read it and could bless others, then feel free to refer it to other people. The purpose of this book is to help you in living an extraordinary life. I believe that God wants this kind of life for all of us.

In the end, I wish to thank you for the contribution that you chose to bring the moment you bought this book. Each copy sold means a donation of 50% of its price towards helping people. You have not only invested in yourself, but also in others, through its purchase. To finish, I would like to encourage you to write about whatever need, help or contentment you have. Your statement and the way in which your life changed as a result of this book, counts, therefore, I am keen to read your story. Feel free to write to me at my email address: alexis.ciuciu@yahoo.com

Thank you!
Yours faithfully,
Alexandru Ciuciu-Freisinger